POST-SOVIET-TYPE ECONOMIES IN TRANSITION

DATE			

Post-Soviet-Type Economies in Transition

JAN WINIECKI

Prepared in collaboration with
Centre for Research into Communist Economies
London

Avebury

Aldershot · Brookfield USA · Hong Kong · Singapore · Sydney

Published by
Avebury
Ashgate Publishing Limited
Gower House
Croft Road
Aldershot
Hants GU11 3HR
England

Ashgate Publishing Company
Old Post Road
Brookfield
Vermont 05036
USA

A CIP catalogue record for this book is available from the British Library and the US Library of Congress.

ISBN 1 85628 406 9

Printed and Bound in Great Britain by
Athenaeum Press Ltd, Newcastle upon Tyne.

Contents

Contents

Introduction

The transition of Eastern Europe, or more precisely of post-Soviet-type economies (post-STEs hereafter) is, as many have stated before, an unprecedented phenomenon. Economic theory did not deal with how to abandon planning in favour of the market. The speed of change in post-STEs adds to the difficulties of both theoretical and empirical analysis.

It is not surprising, then, that the literature on the subject, in spite of its exponential growth, consists largely of conference papers that appear later as proceedings in book format and/or in learned journals. Books by individual authors that deal with the transition, or some of its aspects, in a comprehensive manner have been very few so far. The collection of papers introduced here, written between mid-1990 and early 1992, offers more than the former but less then the latter.

While it is a collection of papers, it does not put the reader off by presenting widely disparate—if not actually conflicting—interpretations of the same or related phenomena. And, although this collection does not offer a comprehensive treatment of all the interrelated issues of transition, it was nonetheless written by a single author. The reader may observe that themes picked up in one article in the collection are developed later at greater length in another. Also, he may, hopefully, discern some coherence in the present writer's views on various aspects of transition in spite of fast changing underlying conditions.

This coherence is reinforced by consistent application of the accumulated knowledge of the economics and the political economy of the Soviet system. In this author's view many of the alleged puzzles of transition, debated in the growing literature on the subject, stem from neglect of this body of knowledge.

It is certainly necessary to apply general economic theory as it evolved in the West in order to grasp the problems of transition and present them in an intelligible form. But it is not sufficient. As I have stressed already, the received theory never envisaged a transition from planned to market economy and therefore is only indirectly applicable.

Nor is it sufficient for clear understanding of post-STEs' problems of transition to treat them as if they were developing countries (LDCs). Even if one puts aside serious doubts about the usefulness of a large part of the body of thinking called development economics (see, e.g., Lal, 1983), there are still many, often striking, differences between the distortions characteristic of LDCs and STEs. The most basic is the difference between distorted and largely non-existent markets (see, i.a., Beksiak, Gruszecki, Jedraszczyk & Winiecki, 1989; Winiecki, 1990).

Thus again, although helpful, comparisons of stabilizations and liberalizations in both sets of countries are not sufficient to understand what has been taking place in the latter. The legacy of the STE past casts a long shadow over the transition to a capitalist market economy (see Winiecki & Winiecki, 1992). Deviations from outcomes expected on the basis of general economic theory, or its applications to LDCs, more often than not stem from the impact of the inherited system-specific features.

This book consist of two parts. In the first the reader will find four papers dealing with stabilization and liberalization. These two components of every transition programme are treated as inseparable. No lasting stabilization is possible without a fairly large degree of liberalization, both internal and external. And no liberalization can succeed, i.e. last for a long enough period to be able to bring about the expected increases in efficiency, without a reasonably stable macroeconomic framework. In the second part there are three papers on privatization and institutional change in general.

Stabilization and Liberalization: Neglect of the STE Past

Chapter 1 deals with the hotly debated phenomenon of the steep fall in output, especially industrial output, in the initial phase of transition (to the tune of 30%-45%) that was registered by all post-STEs undergoing the transition. The extent of the fall was not anticipated by the architects of the so-called 'heterodox' stabilization programme or by the 'Washington Twins' that recommended the programme everywhere. Dramatic fall in output is regarded by many critics as the most important piece of evidence of the failure or, at a minimum, excessive cost of transition.

Although the present writer has often been critical of certain features of the IMF-recommended programme (see Beksiak & Winiecki, 1990; Winiecki, 1991 and Chapter 3 below; Winiecki, 1992), the steep fall in output has little, if anything, to do with the weaknesses for which that programme is criticized. The behaviour of output, it is stressed in Chapter 1, is to a very large degree a consequence of the STE past.

The author points out that the fall in output, and a very sizable one at that, was inevitable with the change from less to more efficient economic system. Apart from eliminating fictitious output, i.e. output registered on the basis of doctored reports, the change - more importantly—eliminated the need to maintain abnormally large inventories. The disappearance of excess demand and the expected tightening of financial discipline *vis-à-vis* state enterprises sharply reduced their precautionary demand for inputs and capital goods. The consequence has been a very sizable output fall.

The extent of that fall may be illustrated with the help of data that did not exist at the time of writing the article that forms the basis of Chapter 1. Rough calculations of the ratio between inventories (overwhelmingly input inventories) and GDP in Poland showed that between 1985 and 1989 it was in the range of 50% to 54% (already lower than in other STEs). This ratio fell dramatically in 1990 to roughly 35%. As enterprises sharply reduced inventories, their new orders plummeted. The foregoing affected intermediate, capital and even consumer goods because consumers also eliminated precautionary purchases that protected them against shortages.

In the light of the above, the fall in industrial output by 24.2% and in GDP by 12% becomes much more understandable. Poland was not the only country that was affected by this one-off downward adjustment. In Czecho-Slovakia, the fall in the first year of the stabilization cum liberalization programme was as severe: in industrial output by 23.1% and in GDP by 16.4%. In East Germany for special reasons the fall was even greater, while in Hungary, also for country-specific reasons, it was spread over a couple of years (but not much smaller in the aggregate).

Interestingly, a knowledge of the Soviet economic system allows the author to explain the output fall not only in terms of macroeconomic aggregates such as inventories and GDP but also in terms of structural distortions. As this author stressed some years ago (Winiecki, 1987 and 1988), STEs displayed over time increasing distortions in the structure of output and employment. In consequence, systemic change of necessity entails a shrinkage of the oversized industrial sector to proportions normally found in market economies at a similar development level (i.e. by about one fourth to one third). This may be easily seen in Figure A. Thus, structural change in post-STEs is accompanied by a fall in the aggregate level of output above all in the oversized industrial sector (on this point see also recently Wijnbergen, 1991).

While Chapter 1 deals with the 'puzzle' of the steep fall in output in general terms, Chapters 2 and 3 cover Polish stabilization

4

Figure A

Changes in the share of industry in GDP and employment in market and Soviet-type economies across the GDP per capita spectrum (trend lines with respect to market economies; assumption-based lines with respect to Soviet-type economies)

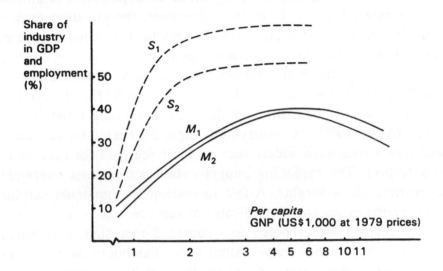

Key: M1 and S1 = share of industry in GDP of market (M) and Soviet-type (S) economies.
M2 and S2 = share of industry in employment.

and liberalization in detail. This concentration on the experience of one country does not, however, mean that the Polish case is a unique one. Many problems considered there are of a more general nature and relevant for other post-STEs in transition.

Even a cursory reading of these two chapters reveals the difference in the author's overall assessment of the Polish transition after the first half of 1990 (Chapter 2) and the first half of 1991 (Chapter 3), the former being definitely more positive. This was the case not only because, in this author's opinion, Polish macroeconomic policy makers made a series of mistakes in the mid-

1990 to early 1991 period. Even more important were increasingly visible consequences of the effects of an IMF-type stabilization programme under the conditions inherited from the STE past.

Moreover, the legacy of the Soviet system interacted with the programme in a very particular—and largely unnoticed—way, with the result of giving the programme an appearance of almost instantaneous success. Over time, however, the situation took a turn for the worse and problems thought to have been solved at the start of the transition resurfaced again.

In mid-1990 the Polish programme looked very well and was widely presented as an example for other post-STEs. Hyperinflation had been stopped, although the 3-5% per month inflation rate since March 1990 was worryingly high. Parallel falls in output and real wages were widely seen as the price paid for success in this respect. The exploding budget deficit was almost overnight converted into a surplus. A fast increasing foreign trade surplus was greeted as yet another indicator of success.

The present writer noted in Chapter 2 that state enterprises (SOEs) were reducing output rather than adjusting to the new conditions of excess supply domestically and higher requirements posed by more demanding markets (see also Wijnbergen, 1991). He also stressed some other output- and trade-related problems looming ahead. But still the success looked more solid in mid-1990 than it turned out to be a year later.

The reasons for that were manifold. Firstly, a monetary squeeze in economies where the property rights structure differs drastically from that assumed in macroeconomic textbooks brings about effects that also differ sharply from those expected. As both banks and industrial enterprises are state-owned, they continue—partly out of inertia—the old pattern of lending and borrowing. Banks do not care much about the creditworthiness of their most important clients, that is large industrial SOEs, while SOEs do not care about the level of interest rate (as they expect to be bailed out anyway).

In consequence, an extended monetary squeeze brings about largely perverse results. As money become scarce, the least efficient giants get their largely unchanged volume of loans, while more efficient medium-sized and smaller SOEs are 'crowded out'. Not only does output then fall by more than necessary, as better enterprises are unable to maintain output or expand, but the output structure deteriorates because the least efficient giants reduce output by less or maintain it in the face of decline in more efficient SOEs. Over time, then, an output fall that was a one-off downward adjustment to a more efficient economic system was superseded or accompanied by a real loss in terms of both output and efficiency.

As this author has written elsewhere, the monetary policy of the standard stabilization programme is therefore in need of adaptation to the system-specific conditions of post-STEs (see Winiecki, 1991 and 1992). Thus, what happened in Poland clearly has wider implications.

Another success fizzled out even more spectacularly—and in a manner that made it intelligible even for non-specialists in the Soviet-type economy. This was the disappearance of the budget surplus toward the end of the first year of transition. The pattern was repeated so far by every post-STE initiating a stabilization programme.

The ease of converting deficit into surplus at the start of transition, a feat rarely achieved elsewhere, was one of the consequences of the STE past. As noted with respect to Chapter 1, enterprises in STEs hoarded excessivly large inventories. With the start of the transition, these inventories bought at low controlled prices were used in output sold at high decontrolled prices. Consequently, high profit rates were achieved in spite of generally rather low capacity utilization levels.

Furthermore, as tax revenue in STEs depended so much on SOEs' profits, tax revenue in Poland (and elsewhere) was correspondingly high. As these windfall profits disappeared over time, SOEs' profitability began to decline and tax revenue declined accordingly. As stressed in Chapter 4, the pattern of diminishing budget deficit was reversed. In other types of countries budget deficits declined rather slowly, given the problems of cutting expenditure. In post-STEs in transition, owing to the legacy of the STE past, they declined very fast only to reappear later on. Again, this has not been confined to Poland; of all the countries of East-Central Europe only Czecho-Slovakia has so far not registered an ever-growing budget deficit.

The least well perceived STE legacy is the one that influenced yet another yardstick of success, namely foreign trade surplus. In earlier liberalizations combined with stabilizations it has been a well observed pattern that after opening up the economy imports rose first, while exports expanded with a lag. This pattern, determined by importers' better knowledge of the domestic market than exporters' knowledge of foreign markets, dictated the need for a stabilization fund. The fund is expected to cover the shortfall of foreign exchange during the period between the rise in imports and in exports.

However, it was hardly noticed that in all post-STEs imports actually fell after the start of transition and that the surplus resulted to a much smaller extent from an increase in exports. What produced that unexpected fall in imports? Again, we have to turn to the STE legacy (as the present author did in Chapter 4). In the first place, hoarding by SOEs did not stop at the border and generally entailed excess demand for imported inputs and machinery as well. In the second, SOEs preferred imports or, to be more precise, imports from the West, to domestic products.

Again, as in the case of generalised hoarding, the threat of an end to the customary lax financial control, forced SOEs to exercise much greater prudence in their choice. Therefore, after the start of transition imports fell and moderate increases in exports were sufficient to produce large surpluses on the trade balance (in fact, a smaller fall in exports than in imports was enough in Czecho-Slovakia in 1991).

However, in a reverse pattern to the one noted in other stabilizing and liberalizing countries, imports began to catch up later. Post-STEs owe these late import surges to the 'heterodox' stabilization programmes and their use of fixed (pegged) exchange rates as yet another inflation anchor. The approach has been criticised by this author in Chapters 3 and 4 as the one that prevents post-STEs in transition from reaping the full benefits of opening up their economies.

As exports become progressively less profitable there is little if any shifting of resources to export sectors. Arbitrary devaluations such as those by the Polish and Hungarian authorities (and in 1990 also by those of the federal government of the former Yugoslavia), are not enough to undo the damage. They may influence current exports but they introduce great uncertainty and consequently reduce the number and value of possible longer term export contracts to a level lower than it otherwise would have been. Nor is the uncertainty conducive to a smooth shift of resources to export sectors.

For the sake of theoretical clarity yet another more general argument should be made against the 'heterodox' stabilization programme with its multiple nominal 'anchors' (quantity of money, exchange rate, wage rate). Mundell (1991) and others (see, e.g., Meltzer, 1992) have underlined the mathematical inconsistency of systems where there is more than one fixed nominal value. From the general equilibrium point of view the system cannot reach stable internal and external equilibrium at full employment (although in our case the overfull employment and structural distortions ensure there will not be employment equilibrium in the short run anyway).

All in all it should not be surprising that the present writer wrote recently that the stabilization programme in question has become a part of the problem for post-STEs in transition, not only part of (or even a key to) the solution (Winiecki, 1992). More to the point, the 'heterodox' programme additionally contributed to the high level of unexpectedness in the transition discussed in the last chapter of Part One.

In Chapter 4 this writer asked a relatively simple, although earlier neglected, question: 'To what extent do the outcomes of the transition so far conform to expectations of theorists and policy makers based on relevant economic theories?' Thence came the attempt to divide evidence into three categories: developments that were expected and did take place accordingly, those that were expected but failed to take place and, finally, those that were not expected but did happen in the process of transition.

The overall assessment in Chapter 4 is unequivocal in its judgement. By far the largest category is the last. Unexpected developments exceed the other in number and, even if some developments took place as expected in almost all cases they could be classified as such only on 'yes but ...' basis. The present writer stressed throughout this introduction and it comes out clearly in Chapter 4 that a consistent application of knowledge of the Soviet economic system would have reduced the number of developments regarded by many analysts as unexpected.

Privatization: Ignorance, Time Factor and Expectations

Part Two of the book concerns institution-building for the market system, with privatization as a linchpin of the whole institutional change. Two chapters out of the three deal exclusively with this all important topic. The answer to the question: 'Why privatization?', when almost no institution of the market seems to be in place in these countries is a straightforward one. The historical evidence of better performance by privately owned firms is overwhelming and, as revealed in the past decade, has become clear to everybody at both intersystemic and intrasystemic levels. Not only the collapse of the Soviet economic system but also the unsatisfactory relative performance of SOEs *vis-à-vis* private firms throughout the Western world (and in many LDCs as well) support the historical evidence.

In Chapter 5 the present writer adds theoretical arguments in favour of private enterprise and, by the same token, of privatisation. He stresses the need to consider the whole spectrum of enterprises differentiated by their property rights characteristics and, then, to compare them according to performance. Thus, he compares such enterprises in terms of their allocational efficiency and their ability to expand the social opportunity set (the range of choices) through innovation. The approach taken in the article upon which Chapter 5 is based is particularly pertinent to practical considerations of post-STE privatization. For it is not only SOEs and privately owned firms that are considered there.

The analysis in question also covers alternatives that are in vogue in various (usually left-wing) quarters in post-STEs and in the West. The results of this comparative enterprise analysis are unequivocal, though. Both labour-managed (self-management) firms and, to a somewhat smaller extent, closed ESOP-type firms are expected to perform worse than private firms with respect to both allocational efficiency and innovativeness. The message stemming from this author's theoretical exercise is clear: it is not just any market economy but a capitalist market economy, with dominant private ownership, that is expected to perform best.

Now, although economic theory tells us that, out of various forms of ownership, private ownership performs best, it tells us little about how to get from where post-STEs are today to an economy with predominantly private ownership. Privatization debates and privatization activities in countries in transition reflect this uncertainty with respect to both goals and means—all the more so as uncertainty is even deeper in post-STEs because their privatization, just like their stabilization, differs greatly from earlier experience in the West and in LDCs.

It differs in scale as it applies to a public sector that amounts to some 80-90% or even 100% of all productive assets. But in contrast to the vast scale, its scope is at the start much narrower than elsewhere. In post-STEs privatization tends to concentrate on industry and agriculture, for it is the dismal performance of goods-producing sectors that contributed to these countries' present morass. Given the enormous problems there, problems with utilities, municipal services, as well as health and education tend to be pushed into the background. All this contrasts with heated debates surrounding these problems in Western privatizations.

Privatization in post-STEs differs also in institutions. The legal framework, established financial markets, as well as trained and experienced players are all in place in Western privatizations. The opposite is, however, the case in post-STEs in transition.

In fact, even the name of the phenomenon, that is 'privatization', is not necessarily adequate for defining what has been taking place in the countries in question. In some post-STEs the ideas of improving the performance of SOEs without changing property rights, long discarded in the West, are still alive and well. Relatively ignorant with respect to Western governments' earlier failed attempts to reorganize, decentralize, commercialize, etc., some left wing collectivist and right wing paternalist believers in the superior role of the state are trying or—at a minimum—suggesting various measures short of privatization.

Given the differences in comparison with what has been taking place elsewhere, it would be presumptuous—to say the least—to offer (as many, unfortunately do!) yet another allegedly guaranteed formula of privatization success. This statement may be said to be the motto of Chapter 6. What the present writer does there is to offer a few suggestions on how to avoid major mistakes. And even where he formulates his opinions in a more positive manner, recommendations stress the need to keep as many options open as possible rather than opt exclusively for some specific (and allegedly miraculous) solution.

The warning against what he called 'capitalism without capitalists' has already been implicit in the theoretical analysis presented in Chapter 5. Property rights theory-based analysis there underlined the importance of the capitalist, i.e. private ownership-based, market system.

Apart from the warning against temptations to heed some 'third road' formula, other warnings by this author concern three issues of critical importance for the privatization process. They are the following: (1) concentration upon the means or methods of privatization before clearly formulating its goal(s); (2) neglect of the time factor; and (3) disregard for the political economy aspect of the process.

The author's critique of Polish privatization strategy illustrates the first warning. The tried and tested British-style privatization through the public offer of shares convinced policy makers of its advantages. This took place without clear thinking about what should be the goals of Polish privatization. The first priority should not be the wide dispersion of shares but the creation of a capitalist class and the closely related issue of efficient control over the management of privatized SOEs. Both required at least a degree of concentration rather than the wide dispersion of ownership implied in the public sale of shares.

Quite clearly, had the thinking about goals preceded that about methods, initial choice—or choices—would have been different. The foregoing was typical of yet another type of error, that of transplantation of methods either unsuited or in need of adaptation to a different institutional environment. In a way, a parallel may be drawn here between the application of the IMF-recommended stabilization programme and British-style privatization. In both cases it was important to adjust standard Western recipies to differing institutions in the post-STE world. As Ohashi (1987) wrote with respect to privatization in the non-Western world, 'innovation and imagination become more important than the analysis of past approaches' (pp.105-106). Few post-STE governments, however, acted imaginatively enough, losing valuable time and public goodwill during the learning process.

This brings us straight to the next major mistake this author warns against in Chapter 6, namely to the underappreciation of the time factor. In this particular respect he agrees with Dornbusch (1990) that it is more important to privatize fast than it is to do it very well. Property rights theory, as well as public choice and collective action theories and Austrian economics, all tell us in no uncertain terms that an economy with predominantly state or other collective ownership is unbalanced almost by definition.

Therefore, as this author wrote elsewhere, 'fast—even if inevitably messy—privatization matters more than a faultless scheme that will take years to formulate and decades accomplish' (Winiecki, forthcoming). However, only Czecho-Slovak policy makers grasped the importance of the time factor right at the start of their transition drive. Their shortcut voucher scheme has largely reflected the view that privatization should be as fast as possible. Other governments corrected their policies only after valuable time was lost and public goodwill dissipated, with detrimental effects for the speed of privatization—and *de facto* transition as a whole.

A related problem, also signaled by the present writer elsewhere (Winiecki, forthcoming), has been the generally over-optimistic assessment of the efficacy and speed of one's own privatization scheme(s). Officials in all post-STEs where transition has been advancing for some time expected their chosen privatization schemes to be implemented both much faster and with much less difficulty than has actually been the case.

The differential between expectations and realities has been at times staggering. In Poland and Hungary the announced annual privatization targets, in some case ran into hundreds of SOEs, while realities reduced these numbers by a factor of ten (or even more). Expectations in the Czecho-Slovak shortcut scheme were also higher but the numbers were reduced by about one third in the first phase of the scheme (from about 2000 SOEs to about 1400). Still, many an obstacle awaited unsuspecting post-STE governments that embarked upon the privatization path.

The last of the three probable major mistakes concerns political aspects of privatization. Since the present writer regards this issue as of particular importance and as such meriting separate treatment (in the next section), he turns to the last recommendation of Chapter 6, based on the recognition of that particularly high degree of ignorance everybody faces in the privatization process. Governments, other public and private economic agents, as well as households, have to cope not only with the usual dose of ignorance inevitably affecting every human action, as taught by Mises and Hayek, but with added doses of ignorance attributable precisely to the unprecedented nature of the process.

Unexpected developments stemming from this source have already proved the point. The long-prepared Polish public sale programme accomplished 10 privatizations in two years, involving SOEs that employed 28,300 workers. In contrast, privatization through liquidation, little thought of at the time of formulating the strategy, involved hundreds of SOEs employing more than twice as many workers. Hungarian privatization through public sale was even less successful, disappointing potential domestic and foreign share buyers.

The architects of the Czecho-Slovak voucher scheme were also surprised by the fact that a majority of voucher holders decided not to exercise their right to buy shares of privatized enterprises in the successive rounds of privatization but placed their vouchers with investment funds. The surprise, however, is largely due to relative ignorance of the pattern of financial asset holding among citizenry in market economies. Czecho-Slovak citizens simply gave evidence to the well known truth that people are generally risk averse and prefer less risky financial assets than shares of joint-stock companies.

Therefore, this author argues in the closing section of Chapter 6 that an unusually high degree of uncertainty suggests the need for post-STE governments to keep their options as open as possible with respect to privatization choices. As the road to success is unknown, simultanous application of a broad range of approaches is preferable. Furthermore, the preference for a range of approaches over 'the one and only' remedy should be extended to prospective approaches as well. The range of options should not be limited to the present ones.

Chapter 7, the last, deals with the broadly conceived institution-building that underpins the transition process. In direct reference to preceding considerations a major conclusion of the chapter is that time emerged as the scarcest factor in the transition process. This does not concern privatisation only. The whole supply of market institutions critically depends on the time needed to put in place institutions aimed at achieving the higher efficiency that is characteristic of the capitalist market system.

Demand for institutions is very high from the start. With supply filling the gap only with the passage of time, a 'workable' or, in other words, tolerably well performing market economy becomes a reality only when and where the gap in question dwindles into insignificance.

There are, however, very serious political economy-type implications of the supply/demand relationship with respect to institutions. For the existence of a large gap between demand for and supply of institutions implies that costs associated with the low efficiency of the economy in transition are front-loaded, i.e. borne in the early transition period, while benefits begin to be felt with a considerable time lag when interdependent institutions of the market have been put in place. This suggests a high probability of social discontent and prospects for political pressure to reduce the costs of transition (on this see the next section of this introduction).

Another theme of Chapter 7 not yet covered by this introductory essay is a differentiation between privatization 'from above' and 'from below' and the differing institutional requirements of each type of privatization. Throughout the literature on the subject it has become customary to understand by the term 'privatization' only the ownership transformation of SOEs. This is privatization 'from above', as the rules of the privatization game and often also the initiative depend on the state.

At the same time growth of the private sector is accomplished also—if not primarily—through the expansion of existing and establishment of new firms that have been privately-owned from the start. This is privatization 'from below', as the decision to expand or start a new business remains with the entrepreneurs.

In post-STEs' transition to the market the attention of policy makers has been concentrated on the former. This applies not only to privatization but to institution-building as a whole. The right to establish private firm has been embodied in law everywhere but the attention span of post-STE governments rarely went beyond this undoubtedly crucial step.

However welcome this embodiment of economic freedom has been, it is only a first step in building institutions for the, overwhelmingly private, small business sector. The emerging small business sector needs banks, insurance companies, venture capital institutions, and many others whose activities should be attuned to the needs of high-risk/small-size firms. And last but certainly not least this entrepreneurial sector needs also financial intermediaries and arrangements that would facilitate takeover of SOEs by private entrepreneurs with a proven record of achievements. For it is in this manner that privatization 'from above' can be supported by that 'from below'. The link-up between the two is also crucial for the larger social and economic goal of speeding up the creation of a capitalist class.

To put it differently, the 'charter of economic freedom' enacted in almost every post-STE creates the possibility for the expansion of the private sector. In order to turn this possibility into a—relatively high—probability, a purposeful institution-building effort is absolutely necessary.

Underappreciated Political Economy of Transition

No article or paper included in the present collection deals specifically with the political economy of transition. The absence of such a paper does not, however, reflect this author's underappreciation of the impact of politics upon systemic transition and economic policy-making. Even in the heady days of the collapse of communist regimes in 1989 and general enthusiasm for political and economic change, he issued a series of warnings in this respect.

These warnings concerned first the 'Solidarity' government's neglect of building popular support for major changes such as privatization (see Beksiak, Eysymontt, Gruszecki, Stankiewicz & Winiecki, 1989). In accordance with this line of reasoning, the present writer stressed at the time (see Beksiak, Gruszecki, Jedraszczyk & Winiecki, 1989, and Beksiak & Winiecki, 1990), as well as today (Winiecki, forthcoming) that the design of the privatization programme should maximize not only economic benefits but also political support.

This aspect of the whole transition programme in post-STEs was by far the worst managed. The promises given were excessively optimistic and were sometimes made in order to ensure short-term acquiescence in painful stabilization measures (such as the Polish government's promise of 'half a year of belt-tightening and then visible improvement'). The price paid for this political short-termism, once the promises of a better future did not materialise, has been rather high.

The problems of post-STE transition stem to an important extent from the fact that improved performance of the economy creating the platform for healthy economic growth—and the resultant growth of household incomes—could not materialise in the short run regardless of government performance. Time is needed to build a network of interdependent institutions that will enable such improved performance to be achieved. This theme has been elaborated in Chapter 7 as well as in some other writings of this author (see, e.g, the transition programme prepared by Beksiak, Gruszecki, Jedraszczyk & Winiecki, 1989).

The reality of privatization pressed home also the initially less obvious problem that even with daring short-cuts, such as the Czecho-Slovak voucher scheme, privatization takes more time than was anticipated. Governments' expectations in this respect tend invariably to be over-optimistic. But without the dominance of private economic agents, the efficiency of the emerging market system is going to be much lower than needed for the expected take-off.

Worse still, not only the institutional component of transition but also its stabilization cum liberalization component tend to concentrate costs in the early phase of transition, while the growth benefits of stable macroeconomic environment can only be reaped in the future. Stabilization measures are always painful since they entail reduction in subsidies and other forms of public expenditure, as well as (often) new taxes. Simultaneously monetary stringency puts other constraints on economic activity.

Unfortunately, in post-STEs that adopted the IMF-recommended variety of stabilization cum liberalization programme, other adverse developments than those listed above also affect the early years of transition. The very serious extra costs of the adverse selection of enterprises when stringent monetary policy is applied under the different ownership structure, have been stressed by this author in Chapters 3 and 4. The effects of another nominal 'anchor', the pegged exchange rate, have also been underlined there.

Altogether, the combined consequences of the STE legacy and the 'heterodox' stabilization programme, often in interaction with one another, generate crisis within the state industrial sector. As this sector's windfall profits disappear and performance does not improve significantly, low budget receipts result in reduction of budget expenditure—in a fiscal crisis.

The political economy consequences are very serious. Resistance to transition within the state industrial sector increases strongly because the complaints of the worst performers are not balanced by successes of better performers among SOEs (as the latter are harder hit than wasteful giants resisting the transition). Thus, the sequence runs from industrial sector crisis to fiscal crisis to political crisis. Not everywhere are things as bad as in Poland but support for transition today in post-STEs is markedly lower than it was in 1989-1990. The 'front-loaded' costs of transition, as stressed in Chapter 7, make this process particularly difficult to handle politically.

Given that, it should have been an imperative for post-STE governments to try to build coalitions in favour of more attractive components of the transition programme. Only one component, i.e. privatization, could conceivably play such a role. Therefore, those governments that stressed free distribution could count on greater support for or—at the very least—lower resistance to change. This political economy issue is highlighted in Chapter 6. Among East European countries most advanced in the transition process, this has been best understood in Czecho-Slovakia.

Thus, although it is the economics of the transition from plan to market that has been drawing the attention of the economics profession, the political economy of the process is increasingly seen as a key to success and therefore a worthy object of study. This is only natural as enthusiastic support for democracy and capitalism in the early days of peaceful revolution is superseded by realistic (or, worse still, surrealistic) assessment of the difficulties and costs of transition—and affected interest groups emerge and make themselves felt in the political area clamouring for higher wages, subsidies, protection, cheap credits, etc.

Acknowledgements

At the end of this introductory essay acknowledgements are in order. All the chapters appeared earlier in various format as articles, book chapters or mimeographed working or discussion papers. Thus, Chapter 1 appeared in *Soviet Studies*, Vol. 43, No. 4, 1991. Chapter 2 appeared in *Weltwirtschaftliches Archiv*, Vol. 126, No. 4, 1990. Chapter 3 appeared as Discussion Paper No. 174 of the Kiel Institute for World Economics in September 1991. Chapter 4 appeared in condensed form in *Banca Nazionale del Lavoro*

Quarterly Review, No. 181, June 1992. Chapter 5 appeared in *Communist Economies and Economic Transformation*, Vol. 3, No.4, 1991. Chapter 6 appeared as a book chapter in *The Emergence of Market Economies in Eastern Europe*, Ch. Clague & G.C. Rausser, eds., Blackwell, Oxford. And, finally, Chapter 7 appeared as a chapter in Privatization, Symposium in Honour of Herbert Giersch, Horst Siebert, ed., Institut für Weltwirtschaft an der Universität Kiel, J.C.B. Mohr (Paul Siebeck), Tübingen, 1992. I would like to express my appreciation to all the editors and publishers who allowed me to reproduce the material in this collection.

Materials contained in most of the chapters appeared earlier either as conference papers or as working papers of various academic institutions. I would like in this respect to thank in particular the Kiel Institute for World Economics and the Federal Institute for East European and International Studies in Cologne for the hospitality extended to me during my stay at both institutions.

References

Beksiak, J., Eysymontt, J., Gruszecki, T., Stankiewicz, T. & Winiecki, J. (1989), *Polityczne nastepstwa niektorych planowanych posuniec programu rzadowego* (Political Consequences of Certain Planned Measures in the Government Programme), Warsaw, December, mimeo.

Beksiak, J., Gruszecki, T., Jedraszczyk, A. & Winiecki, J. (1989), *Zarys programu stabilizacyjnego i zmian systemowych* (Outline of a Programme for Stabilization and Systemic Change). Prepared at the request of the Parliamentary Club of 'Solidarity', Warsaw, September, mimeo.

Beksiak, J. & Winiecki, J. (1990), 'A Comparative Analysis of Our Programme and the Polish Government Programme', in: *The Polish Transformation: Programme and Progress*, Centre for Research into Communist Economies, London.

Dornbusch, R. (1991), *Priorities of Economic Reform in Eastern Europe and the Soviet Union*, M.I.T., December 29, mimeo.

Lal, D. (1983), *The Poverty of Development Economics*, Institute of Economic Affairs, London.

Meltzer, A.H. (1992), 'Prices and Wages in Transition to a Market Economy', the Karl Brunner Symposium on Liberty, Analysis and Ideology, June 8-12, Interlaken, mimeo.

Ohashi, T.M. (1987), 'Marketing State-Owned Enterprises', in: *Privatization and Development*, ed. by S. Hanke, International Center for Economic Growth, San Francisco.

Wijnbergen, S. van (1991), *Growth and Economic Reform in Poland: An Outline of the Issues*, World Bank, December, mimeo

Winiecki, E. & Winiecki, J., *The Structural Legacy of the Soviet-Type Economy*, A Collection of Papers, Centre for Research into Communist Economies, London.

Winiecki, J. (1987), 'The Overgrown Industrial Sector in Soviet-Type Economies: Explanations, Evidence, Consequences', *Comparative Economic Studies*, Vol. 28, No. 4.

Winiecki, J. (1988), *The Distorted World of Soviet-Type Economies*, Routledge, London.

Winiecki, J. (1990), 'Privatisation in Communist Countries: Crucial Differences and Problems', *Economic Affairs*, Vol. 10, No. 4.

Winiecki, J. (1991), 'The Polish Transition Programme at Mid-1991: Stabilization under Threat', Kiel Discussion Paper 174, Kiel Institute for World Economics, September, mimeo.

Winiecki, J. (1992), 'Monetary Perversity in Post-Soviet Economies', *Wall Street Journal*, February 6.

Winiecki, J., forthcoming, *Privatization in Poland. A Comparative Perspective*, J. C. B. Mohr (Paul Siebeck), Tübingen.

Part One

Stabilizing and Liberalizing Post-Soviet-Type Economies

1 Pitfalls on the way to the market: The mystery of vanishing output

The steep fall in industrial output in Poland and the even steeper one in East Germany at the start of the respective transition programmes came as a surprise to many analysts. It prompted a discussion on the 'costs of transition', giving the chance to criticise the 'big bang' (or 'shock therapy' or 'critical mass') approach by both residual believers in the old order and proponents of various allegedly painless formulae of gradual transition.

Leaving aside the discussion itself, I shall concentrate here on the fall in output and its treatment as a cost of transition to the market. What is particularly puzzling is the near-complete neglect of the economic theory of the centrally planned (or centrally administered or Soviet-type) economy in discussion of the fall in output in the early stages of the transition period. I posit that both economic theory and empirical data supporting that theory clearly suggest exactly such an outcome after the start of the 'big bang'.

I posit further that the fall in output can only to a certain extent be seen as a cost of transition, understood as a welfare loss. A major part of the fall in output has no impact on the welfare of the population. As the economic system changes, so does the behaviour of economic agents: firms and households. The change in behaviour inevitably induces a fall in output but the level of welfare remains unchanged.

In this chapter, first, various sources of output loss are considered and their theoretical rationale is presented. Next, implications of output loss for welfare are presented in comparative economic systems' terms. Finally, policy implications are drawn.

Loss of Non-Existent Output

This somewhat puzzling title, more reminiscent of a mystery story than scholarly analysis, is none the less very precise: one of the sources of the fall in output is the fact that the transition to the market changes radically the structure of incentives. The first casualty is an incentive to cheat.

In the Soviet-type economy agency costs (in the terms of Jensen & Meckling, 1976)—i.e. costs of control by the owner, that is the state—over managers of state enterprises are enormous. On the one hand, a highly pronounced non-exclusiveness of property rights gives rise to various forms of opportunistic behaviour by agents. On the other hand, these opportunities to shirk, steal and cheat are magnified by what this author has called 'measurement without markets' (Szymanderski & Winiecki, 1989; Winiecki, 1991). Since managers are paid by what they report to their superiors and not by what they sell on the market the temptation to cheat is very great. The clear understanding that detection of a doctored report is rather difficult transforms temptation into reality.

Every Russian knows the word *pripiski*. In loose translation it means 'write-ins', that is plan fulfillment figures written into the report that are higher than the real ones. The extent of the phenomenon is, for obvious reasons, difficult to estimate. However, an audit of a few hundred enterprises in the Soviet Union in the early 1980s found every third enterprise guilty of *pripiski* (Shitov, 1981). Now, if every third enterprise covered by that audit was caught making 'write-ins' of one sort or another, it may be safely assumed that the share of those practising the art is much higher.

26

It is quite obvious to the present writer that the fall in output in what used to be the German Democratic Republic stems to some extent from the foregoing phenomenon (in Poland a large part of output was already sold on the market before the 'big bang'). Once enterprises begin to depend on what they sell rather than write to their superiors, a few percentage points of 'output that was not' disappear from statistics—that is, from the only place they existed. This is going to happen in every Soviet-type economy as it shifts to the market system. Also, the greater the extent of hierarchy-related incentives over market-related incentives, i.e. the greater the agency costs, the larger the percentage of output that is going to disappear from statistics.

However, the doctoring of reports to planning authorities in order to earn premiums does not end with such crude tricks as writing into these reports figures taken straight out of thin air. Over the decades of the Soviet-type economy's existence managers refined various methods of obtaining pecuniary benefits within the existing structure of incentives (with its extremely high agency costs).

Received theory of the Soviet-type economy recognises many such methods, of which hidden changes in output structure are of major importance here. Following Csikos-Nagy (1975), Winiecki (1982, 1986a, 1988), Pindak (1983) and others, three categories of manipulative practices can be enumerated.

(1) Changes in the product mix that increase the weight of higher priced substitutes in the output of an enterprise. Increased total output value allows the planned output target to be fulfilled more easily.

(2) Changes (adverse) in product quality through the use of sub-standard materials without a corresponding price reduction. This makes it easier to fulfil the planned profit target (and, if substandard inputs are more easily available, the planned output targets too).

(3) Introduction of pseudo-novelties, i.e. products whose price is increased disproportionately in relation to minor improvements in product characteristics compared with the standard product (usually accompanied by discontinuation or sharp reduction in output of the latter). Higher price and higher value added make it easier to fufil both planned output and profit targets.

Obviously, these manipulative practices are possible in the long run only in a closed economy with persistent excess demand on all markets, such as is characteristic for the Soviet-type economy. Elsewhere, producing, say, 10,000 costly lamps instead of 100,000 inexpensive ones would be a one-off affair. Stocks of unsold lamps would accumulate, while competitors would supply inexpensive lamps in the quantitites demanded, and the financial situation of the enterprise concerned would deteriorate.

However, in the Soviet-type economy managers of other enterprises would not bother to change their respective output mixes because this entails extra effort without extra compensation (they would fulfil plan targets anyway!). Buyers, not finding less expensive lamps, would in most cases be forced to buy more costly ones. Then, if for some reasons they did not buy more expensive lamps—or did not for the time being—the support of the politico-economic hierarchy for state enterprises in financial troubles, known in the economic theory of the Soviet-type economy as the 'soft' budget constraint (Kornai, 1979), would allow the enterprise to survive—and its management to prosper.

Now, the transition to the market begins with tight macroeconomic policy that aims not only at the elimination of disequilibrium inherited from the past but also—in fact first of all—at the realignment of the supply and demand relationship. With a positive real interest rate (for the first time since the beginning of central planning!) and cuts in subsidies in the state budget, demand falls markedly and so does output. The sellers' market, a permanent feature of the Soviet-type economy, disappears or is seriously weakened.

The discipline of the market is felt for the first time by suppliers, who begin to search for customers. This entails changing the output mix so as to increase the saleability of their products in recession. Thus, for example, steel mills, rather than producing as few sizes and grades of steel products as possible (typical in the past), try to enlarge their product variety to get orders (a phenomenon reported in Poland recently). The foregoing involves, however, a change from producing thicker and heavier to thinner and lighter sheet and other steel products, generally neglected under the conditions of persistent sellers' market (it was up to the users to bear the costs of adapting what was produced to their needs). Also, if domestic suppliers will not adjust, foreign suppliers will under the liberalised import regime.

It should be noted, however, that such adjustment means less output; 10,000 thicker steel sheets amounted to more output than the same number of thinner sheets. The same applies to pseudo-novelties. In order to sell at all, enterprises are often forced to shift back to less expensive standard products, cutting back on the more costly pseudo-novelties that would end up in warehouses and, without the 'soft' budget constraint, would threaten the very survival of the enterprises. Although not so immediately as with *pripiski*, the forced abandonment of such practices would be registered as a fall in output in aggregate statistics.

One-Off Downward Adjustment of Output under the Regime Change

The transition to the market system forces economic agents to adjust their behaviour to the changed 'rules of the game', and this behavioural adjustment inevitably results in a fall in output. Again, the theory of the Soviet-type economy is helpful in explaining the determinants of these developments.

Almost 30 years ago Grossman stressed the Sisyphean nature of Soviet central planners' efforts to maintain the semblance of bal-

Table 1.1

Structure of Inventories in Industry in Selected Soviet-type and Market Economics

		Share of total stocks in industry			
(1)	Year (2)	Raw materials purchased intermediate products, fuels, etc. (3)	Unfinished production, produced intermediate products (4)	Spare parts for equipment (5)	Finished products goods for resale (6)
Czecho-Slovakia	1981	64.5	21.3	n.d.[a]	10.4
Hungary	1976	n.d.	n.d.	n.d.	11.9
Poland	1970	63.0	21.0	n.d.[a]	15.1
	1980	63.5	24.5	n.d.[a]	12.0
	1983	62.9	23.2	n.d.[a]	13.9
Soviet Union	1970	59.3	22.3	3.9	14.6
	1980	57.7	23.5	4.9	14.3
GDR	1963	n.d.	n.d.	n.d.	15.4
Austria	1976	n.d.	n.d.	n.d.	32.1
Canada	1970	n.d.	n.d.	n.d.	31.3
Japan	1975	n.d.	n.d.	n.d.	53.2
Sweden	1977	n.d.	n.d.	n.d.	38.2

[a] Included in column (3)

Source: Winiecki, 'Distorted macroeconomics ...'

ance in the economy in the absence of markets and scarcity prices (Grossman, 1963). Over the years, these problems were further elaborated on the basis of microeconomic approaches pointing out the insatiable demand of enterprises under the 'soft' budget constraint and supplier's behaviour with respect to quantity and quality on the seller's market (Kornai, 1980, 1986).

Since the enterprises are continually buffeted by shortages, deliveries of inputs of the wrong type (size, grade) and quality, or by late deliveries or shortages pure and simple, uncertainty reigns supreme (Winiecki, 1986b, 1988). Enterprises react to the foregoing by pursuing strategies that minimise the risk of not fulfilling planned targets and making excessive demands for everything—from inputs to production factors. Hoarding strategies further aggravate shortages and create more uncertainty.

Another consequence of excess demand, shortages and uncertainty is an extremely high level of input inventories. The striking differences between the structure of inventories in Soviet-type and market economies are shown in Table 1.1. Hoarding of labour and capital is less easily estimated but there is a lot of anecdotal (meaning non-systematic) evidence in this respect.

It should have been quite obvious that behavioural traits of Soviet-type economy enterprises would change with the transition to a less wasteful system (and that with this change would come downward adjustment in demand). This is what happened in Poland after 1 January 1990.

Some non-systematic evidence is worth quoting. Thus, to give an example, in the 1980s the Polish controlled press revealed that the Warsaw car factory (FSO) had brought in some parts from a supplier in Szczecin (about 500 km) by helicopter—in order to fulfil plan targets and obtain related premiums and bonuses. The horrendous costs were as usual borne by (domestic) consumers.

Such striking cases of wastefulness are none the less rare (hence the interest of the press), but it has been quite normal for enterprises in the Soviet-type economy to send their own vans, lorries, etc., to bring in small quantities of missing parts and components from negligent suppliers. For that very reason every enterprise tried to have as large a transport fleet of its own as it was possible to obtain (regardless of cost, which mattered little under the 'soft' budget constraint).

After 1 January 1990, with the realignment of the supply and demand relationship under way, suppliers themselves began to search for customers. Understanding this, Polish enterprises cut orders for transport equipment sharply. In contrast with the developments considered in the preceding section, this is a *real* fall in output, not a purely statistical one. Moreover, in the short run this cannot be compensated by marketing output elsewhere because the uncompetitiveness of the Polish economy (and other post-Soviet-type economies) makes it almost impossible to sell these goods on the world market, or forces producers to sell there at a heavy discount. Thus, the one-off downward adjustment in demand by domestic enterprises is inevitably translated into a fall in output.

The case of transport equipment is not unique for the early transition period of the Polish economy. The same thing happened across the whole range of capital and intermediate goods. With respect to the former another telling example is that of metal-working machinery, which experienced a similar sharp fall in domestic demand. Again, this should have been expected on the basis of the received theory, i.e. uncertainty and hoarding behaviour.

Since both maintenance of productive equipment by its producers and supplies of related instruments are notoriously uncertain, all enterprises keep a variety of metal-working machines to make up for that particular system-specific deficiency. Now, if a machine breaks down or some instruments are unavailable (or deliveries are late), managers trying to prevent the non-fulfillment of planned output targets often decide to have them manufactured internally. The costs of such in-house manufacturing of unique or short-series pieces are staggering. In the USSR it was calculated that instruments produced in user enterprises cost 200% to 1,000% more than those manufactured by specialised enterprises; furthermore, the number of metal-working machines in the USSR amounts to 1.9 million, that is, more than there are operators in the country as a whole (see source quoted in Winiecki, 1988). Not surprisingly, the managers of many Polish enterprises decided that under the new economic regime they neither need to expand their metal-working machinery nor can they afford such expansion any more.

I have already stressed the excessive input inventories held by Soviet-type enterprises. Here, adjustment has also been inevitable as the regime changed. Only it was not instantaneous: new orders

32

for inputs are being spread over a longer period, while Polish enterprises began to run down their excessive inventories. Input inventories in industry that increased by 20.8% in 1989 over 1988 in real terms (even for a Soviet-type economy this was an extremely high figure, indicating some additional policy mistakes see Winiecki, 1990), fell in the first quarter of 1990 by 7.8% in real terms.

We have seen how one-off downward adjustment of output affected capital and intermediate goods producers as a result of the changing behaviour of the (state) enterprise sector. However, such adjustment affected consumer goods producers as well, and again this is what theory leads us to expect.

Behaviour of households has also been strongly influenced by the Soviet-type economic system. (The best source on their behaviour under shortage conditions is Kornai, 1980). Food products are the best example. Decades of shortages taught households to make excessively large purchases wherever they could since they did not know when they would be able to make the next purchase of comparable quality and variety. Some fraction of that food was later spoiled in domestic refrigerators.

The supply and demand realignment changed households' behaviour in this respect immediately. I stress 'immediately' because it should be remembered that households—in contrast to state enterprises—never enjoyed a 'soft' budget constraint. Consequently, they had been better trained to react in a cost-minimising manner. Thus, with the disappearance of shortage, excessive, 'precautionary' purchases disappeared as well. This fall in domestic demand for food in the short run has inevitably been translated into a fall in output because there were only very limited possibilities of marketing food products on the world market. The low quality of a large part of Polish and other East European food products (as well as their low sanitary, environmental, etc., standards) makes them unsaleable not only in the short but also in the medium run.

Efficiency Gains from Systemic Change Reduce Welfare Losses

The combined effects of purely statistical output losses and real output losses resulting from the one-off downward adjustment of demand under the market system may be quite substantial, and it should be kept in mind that they are topped by output losses resulting from the initial macroeconomic squeeze associated with the start of the transition programme (the 'big bang').

It is worth stressing that the fall in demand and the subsequent fall in output resulting from restrictive macroeconomic policy is *the only one* that actually reduces welfare. This is, in fact, a cost of transition—the price to be paid for changing the supply and demand relationship and the behaviour of economic agents, enterprises and households.

In contrast, other output losses do not reduce welfare. The disappearance of 'output that was not', analysed in the first section, leaves everything unchanged, except statistics. More importantly, real output losses stemming from transitional downward adjustment of demand do not adversely affect welfare, either. Reduced demand for production factors and production inputs by enterprises, as well as the elimination of 'precautionary' purchases of consumer goods by households, are manifestations of lower use of inputs per unit of either production or consumption made possible by the shift from a less to a more efficient economic system.

It is interesting to note that although the majority of theorists stress the extremely high wastefulness of the Soviet-type economy, very few have combined these findings with expectations of a fall in output resulting from a market system-related efficiency increase. Only exceptionally does one find the clearly formulated view that output 'would fall and should fall' because these economies, on the whole, 'produce goods, valued at about 10% of the GSP, that go straight into inventories never to reappear', as well as install a lot of underused or unused productive capacity (quotations from Sirc, 1990). Sirc stressed also that the fall in output of this sort does not reduce welfare because this part of gross social product 'does not include anything that could be consumed'; on the contrary, it releases resources for healthier economic growth.

This non-equivalence of output and welfare losses has been tentatively confirmed empirically in the case of the Polish transition programme. Both real wage data and food industry sales data registered a fall in the 30%-40% range in the first half of 1990 relative to the December 1989 level. However, household expenditure surveys did not confirm the extent of the fall. Food consumption, according to an April 1990 survey, was estimated to have been only 11% lower than the previous December (Institute of Finance, 1990).

My final concern here is the policy implications of the downward adjustment of demand and fall in output and their relation to the level of welfare. These policy implications can be decomposed into those for economic policy and, somewhat surprisingly at first sight, those for social policy.

The former are much more unequivocal. Since the fall in demand and, subsequently, in output is an inevitable consequence of the regime change, then stimulative demand management policies are at the very least useless. For the only increase in output expected in the early stages of transition may come from microeconomic adjustment of more flexible producers able to find new markets for their products. However, for reasons of weak competitiveness, this is not going to improve the situation markedly in the short run, as we have seen.

The short-run effects of macroeconomic stimulation—which so many are demanding now in Poland—would be primarily if not exclusively on prices. The longer-run effects would be even more pernicious, though. The one-off downward adjustment of demand explained in the preceding section eliminates only the most visible layer of waste. Other efficiency gains are realised in the longer run, when domestic producers adjust further under pressure of both reduced domestic demand and increased international competition (trade liberalisation effect). These adjustments involve

35

quality improvements, increases in the innovation rate (abysmally low under the Soviet-type economic system), improved marketing capabilities and after-sale servicing, etc.

In contrast to the short-run adjustment, they do not necessarily involve a fall in output because enterprises may have enough time to introduce the changes that are necessary for survival in the transition period. (It should be noted in passing that privatisation, by assigning property rights more precisely and reducing agency costs, is expected to improve enterprises' performance.)

However, stimulative macroeconomic policies may slow down this process by supporting the traditional structure of domestic demand and therefore reducing pressure to adjust. The beneficial effects of higher efficiency will then be lower than with a neutral macroeconomic stance.

Recommendations with respect to social policy concern the distributional implications of the output loss caused by regime change. Cries of anguish coming from Poland and from what used to be the German Democratic Republic do not all stem from misunderstanding of the reality or from some kind of heritage of real socialism's fascination with output figures (no matter how fictitious).

Although the output loss due to demand adjustment does not affect the aggregate welfare of the population, the distribution of the income loss resulting from the fall in output is markedly uneven. Those laid off or made redundant pay the highest price for the adjustment to higher efficiency levels. Thus, it should be stressed that the consequences of the fall in output which we have analysed are a social problem that should be dealt with by *social policy* measures (safety net measures), not an economic problem to be dealt with by economic policy measures.

References

Csikos-Nagy, B. (1975), *Socialist Price Theory and Price Policy*, Akademiai Kiado, Budapest.

Grossman, G. (1963), 'Notes for a Theory of the Command Economy', *Soviet Studies*, 15, October.

Institute of Finance (1990), 'Raport o sytuacji finansowej w czerwcu i w pierwszym pólroczu 1990', Warsaw, Instytut Finansów, 30 July, mimeo.

Jensen, M.C. & Meckling, W.H. (1976), 'Theory of the Firm: Managerial Behavior, Agency Costs and Ownership Structure', *Journal of Financial Economics*, 3, 4.

Kornai, J. (1979), 'Resource-Constrained Versus Demand-Constrained Systems', *Econometrica*, 47, 4.

Kornai, J. (1980), *Economics of Shortage*, North-Holland, Amsterdam.

Kornai, J. (1986) 'Soft Budget Constraint', *Kyklos* 39, 1.

Pindak, F. (1983), 'Inflation under Central Planning', *Jahrbuch der Wirtschaft Osteuropas*, 2.

Shitov, A. (1981), 'Povyshenie planovoi distsipliny: trebovanie vremeni', *Planovoe khozyaistvo*, 11.

Sirc, L. (1990), 'Markets Spell Disaster?', in: *The Polish Transformation: Programme and Progress*, Centre for Research into Communist Economies, London.

Szymanderski, J. & Winiecki, J. (1989), 'Dissipation de la rente, managers et travailleurs dans la système soviétique: les implications pour un changement du systeme', *Revue d'Etudes Comparatives Est-Ouest*, 20.

Winiecki, J. (1982), 'Investment Cycles and an Excess Demand Inflation in Planned Economies: Sources and Processes', *Acta Oeconomica*, 28, 1-2.

Winiecki, J. (1986a), 'Open, Hidden and Repressed Inflation under Central Planning: An Overview', *Rivista Internazionale di Scienze Economiche*, 33, 10-11.

Winiecki, J. (1986b), 'Distorted Macroeconomics of Central Planning', *Banca Nazionale del Lavoro Quarterly Review*, 157, June.

Winiecki, J. (1988), *The Distorted World of Soviet-Type Economies* , Routledge, London.

Winiecki, J. (1990), 'Post-Soviet-Type Economies in Transition. What Have We Learned from the Polish Transition Programme in Its First Year', *Weltwirtschaftliches Archiv*, 126, 4.

Winiecki, J. (1991), *Resistance to Change in the Soviet Economic System*, Routledge, London.

2 Poland: Good start at the macrobalance level

Introduction

The transition from the Soviet-type economy (STE for short) to a market-type economy (MTE for short) is an unprecedented endeavour. Therefore, there is a need to delineate clearly the scope of the present analysis. First, it has been stressed that an STE leaves an imprint on the behaviour of economic agents (see, i.a., Winiecki, 1986; 1988). Thus, we should look at the behaviour of households and enterprises under the—largely—changed rules of the game and different macroeconomic conditions.

Next, changed rules and government policies applying these rules should be taken into account. Under the STE regime, government 'hands-on' policy usually added to the system-generated uncertainty (e.g., Grossman, 1963; Kornai, 1979; 1980; Winiecki, 1982; 1986; 1988). Thus, not only the clarity of rules and their efficiency but government's own judgement should become an area of analysis. An inquiry into certain unique phenomena of the transition process itself (i.e., demand behaviour) will follow the policy analysis.

Finally, since stabilisation is a necessary ingredient of transition rather than an end in itself, the relationship between stabilisation and liberalization *cum* privatization should be considered as well.

For only the latter may bring about a fundamental rather than a forced adjustment of the economy. Thus, it is worth seeing whether there are any lessons to be drawn from the existence—or nonexistence—of such a relationship. Closing remarks deal with the more general question whether there exists only the one sequence of stabilisation, liberalization, and privatization for countries shifting from STE to MTE regime.

A Brief Round-Up of the Performance of the Polish Economy in the First Half of 1990

The Government transition programme had to accomplish two types of goals. The first was the goal of stabilizing an economy in which price increases bordered on hyperinflation in the second half of 1989, while the budget deficit reached some 10% of GDP at the end of the third quarter of that year. Therefore, the programme entailed both a restrictive monetary policy and an attempt at balancing the budget. Wage controls in the form of punitive wage taxes imposed upon the enterprises' wage bill exceeding a certain (very low) level of compensation for price increases were aimed at both the already ongoing inflationary spiral and the expected new additions to inflation (effects of liberalisation of those prices that were still controlled by the state).

The second goal was that of liberalising the Polish economy. The most important measures were domestic price liberalisation and the introduction of a limited currency convertibility. Both measures, coupled with the elimination of a large part of subsidies, created a strong inflationary impulse.

In the first month of the programme, prices by and large doubled (Table 2.1), but thereafter the rate of price changes declined sharply as enterprises encountered a barrier of steeply falling demand for their products. In the third month of the programme, inflation was already at the 5% rate per month. In comparison with near-hyperinflation in the preceding period of still partly controlled prices, this was an unqualified success. However, the inflation rate did not decline further in the next three months.

Industrial output contracted sharply at the beginning of 1990 and stabilized at a low level during the first half of 1990. Official statistics are given in Table 2.1, although there are disputes as to how low that level might be, given the statistical inadequacies. Unemployment has been slowly creeping up but is nowhere near the level commensurate with the fall in output.

Levels of capacity utilization fell and remained low, as would have been expected with the sharp contraction of output and its

Table 2.1

Monthly Basic Indicators: Prices and Quantities in 1990

Month	Consumer price index	Industrial output	Industrial empl.	Exports[b]	
		Preceding month = 100			
Jan	178.6	68.4	98.9	30.1	
Feb	123.9	98.0	99.0	224.2	
Mar	104.7	100.9	99.0	132.5	
Apr	108.1	98.4	99.0	82.3	
May	105.0	100.1	98.2	108.9	
Jun	103.4	103.9	99.2		
	Consumer price index	Industrial output[a]	Industrial empl.	Trade balance	
				($ mill.)	(per cent of exports)
		December 1989 = 100			
Jan	178.6	68.4	98.9	25	7.4
Feb	221.3	67.0	97.9	257	24.9
Mar	231.7	67.6	96.9	778	38.4
Apr	250.5	66.5	95.9	1,209	41.8
May	263.0	66.6	94.2	1,605	42.7
Jun	269.8	70.3	93.5	2,077	44.5

[a] Mining, manufacturing, and electricity in state sector in comparable working time.
[b] In convertible currencies (excl. exports to the USSR and other STEs).

Source: Materials of Central Statistical Office, National Bank of Poland, and Ministry of Finance.

later stagnation. What, however, remained a puzzle for both domestic and foreign observers of the Polish scene was the continuously high profitability in spite of the sharply reduced output. In spite of all the complaints about high interest rates (monthly rediscount rates, see Table 2.2), taxes, etc., state enterprises survived

Table 2.2

Monthly Monetary Indicators, December 1989 - June 1990

Month	Money supply[a]			Discount rate (nominal)
	trillion zlotys	nominal growth (Dec 1989 = 100)	real growth[b]	(% on a monthly basis)
Dec 89	26.4	100.0	100.0	X
Jan 90	37.3	141.3	79.3	36
Feb 90	45.3	171.6	77.5	20
Mar 90	55.1	208.7	90.0	10
Apr 90	62.0	234.9	93.8	8
May 90	70.4	266.6	102.0	5.5
Jun 90	77.9	295.1	109.4	4
	Domestic credit expansion[c]			Discount rate (real)[d]
	trillion zlotys	nominal growth (Dec 1989=100)	real growth[d]	(% on a monthly basis)
Dec 89	30.7	100.0	100.0	X
Jan 90	33.0	107.5	51.2	- 35.2
Feb 90	38.3	124.6	53.8	8.8
Mar 90	44.8	145.9	63.4	10.6
Apr 90	57.0	185.7	79.7	6.7
May 90	63.5	206.8	88.4	5.1
Jun 90	69.4	226.1	94.8	2.6

[a] Notes and coins in circulation, households' demand and time deposits, and enterprises' deposits.
[b] Deflated by the consumer price index from Table 2.1.
[c] Credits extended to state enterprises, households, private enterprises and farmers.
[d] Deflated by the wholesale price index, since an overwhelming part of credits has been extended to state enterprises.

Source: See Table 2.1

Table 2.3

Households' Incomes, Expenditures and Money Holdings in Nominal and Real Terms (December 1989=100)

Month	Incomes		Retail sales[a]		Money holdings[b]	
	nominal	real[c]	nominal	real[c]	nominal	real[c]
Dec 89	100.0	100.0	100.0	100.0	100.0	100.0
Jan 90	139.1	77.9	109.7	61.4	120.2	67.3
Feb 90	145.9	65.9	112.9	51.0	191.6	82.8
Mar 90	174.4	75.3	126.9	54.8	191.6	82.7
Apr 90	175.9	70.2	152.7	61.0	214.6	85.7
May 90	174.4	66.3	159.1	60.5	234.3	89.1
Jun 90	215.6	79.9	164.8	61.1	250.5	92.8

[a] In state retail outlets only.
[b] Cash holdings as well as domestic currency demand and time deposits of households.
[c] Deflated by the consumer price index.

Source: See Table 2.1

the first half of 1990 in a surprisingly good financial condition and without the expected bankruptcies.

A turnaround of historical proportions occurred in 1990 in the supply/demand relationship. For the first time since the imposition of central planning on the Polish economy, generalised excess supply on both consumer and producer goods markets emerged. This has been regarded as another unqualified success of the transition programme. According to received theory, producers have been forced to adjust.

Some adjustment did occur. Beginning in March, exports to countries with convertible currencies began to exceed those in the respective months of 1989 and in the first five months of 1990 were 10.8% higher than in the corresponding period of 1989. However, the absolute size of the trade surplus was deceptively large because imports fell by 31.1% in the same period.

Households were very severely hit by the stabilisation programme. Real wages decreased by 24% in January and a further 16.8% in February 1990 and later began to increase, slowly and unevenly. Data on incomes are shown in Table 3.

These developments had their obvious feedback effect on consumer goods industries. Moreover, the government budget was kept in balance (another measure of success), but this was achieved by raising revenues rather than cutting expenditure.

Work on privatization started in September 1989. However, no privatisation took place at first, and the bill was hotly contested in Parliament, with an alternative draft submitted by a group of left-leaning MPs. The latter preferred self-management and employee stock ownership (ESOP).

The government did not move fast to end various monopolies. Many critics think that the government yielded too much to vested interests trying to protect their rents. This attitude has been displayed both with respect to the communist *nomenklatura* and to 'Solidarity' allies (a satellite peasant party that switched sides after the 1989 elections).

Household Behaviour

Both in the period of accelerating inflation and in the period of the sharp fall in real wages that began in late 1989 and accelerated in the first months of the transition, Polish households behaved in a textbook manner. First, with the acceleration of inflation they markedly increased the share of cash in the money stock they held: from 22-32% in 1986-87 (already a large share and typical for a high-inflation country) to 38% in 1988 and still more in 1989. In the last three months of that year the share of cash exceeded 50%.

Second, they tried to get rid of money holdings by advancing purchases of durables and—in the last months before the 'big bang'—also of non-durables. The changes in cash balances are shown in Table 2.4.

Third, they shifted to less depreciating assets (mostly to convertible currency holdings). The share of savings in domestic currency fell from three fourths in 1985 to one third of the total in

Table 2.4

Households' Cash Balances, 1985-89 and January-June 1990

	Cash balances trillion zlotys	Incomes	Cash balance incomes ratio
1985	0.9	5.6	0.16
1986	1.1	6.9	0.16
1987	1.2	8.7	0.14
1988	2.4	16.0	0.15
1989	8.9	71.9	0.12
Jan 90	10.5	18.5 (222)[a]	0.05
Feb 90	(11.1)[b]	19.4 (233)[a]	0.06
Mar 90	(14.7)[b]	23.2 (278)[a]	0.07
Apr 90	(18.9)[b]	23.4 (281)[a]	0.08
May 90	(22.1)[b]	23.2 (278)[a]	0.08
Jun 90	24.2	25.9 (311)[a]	0.08

[a] Monthly incomes multiplied by 12.
[b] Notes and coins outside bank vaults, including, however, cash balances of enterprises (usually 5-10% of the total).

Source: See Table 2.1

1989. The process accelerated towards the end of that year (by end-December 1989 domestic currency holdings amounted to a meagre 11%. Data are shown in Table 2.5.

After the 'big bang' and a heavy fall in real wages, households tried to smooth the adjustment to a lower consumption level by drawing on their convertible currency holdings in January and February. The cutting down came to a halt in the first half of 1990 and the process of rebuilding convertible currency holdings is slow—much slower than the process of rebuilding money holdings in domestic currency to their normal level although, considering the highly unstable 1980s (unstable even for STEs), it is difficult to say what that 'normal' level might be. On the one hand, the cash balances/incomes ratio fell by 20% in 1989 relative to the 1985-88 period, as can be seen from Table 2.4, and this process continued in early 1990. On the other hand, savings in nominal terms increased markedly faster than incomes in nominal terms. In real terms, the latter fell by 30.2% in the first half of

44

Table 2.5

Structure of Savings in Domestic and Convertible Currencies, 1985-89 and January-June 1990

| | In domestic currency | | In convertible currencies[a] | |
	trillion zlotys	% of total	trillion zlotys	% of total
1985	1.7	74	0.6	26
1986	2.1	65	1.1	35
1987	2.5	50	2.5	50
1988	3.8	32	8.1	68
1989	8.6	34	16.7	66
Dec 89	8.6	11	68.6[b]	89
Jan 90	11.0	16	60.0[b]	84
Feb 90	13.6	19	57.7[b]	81
Mar 90	16.5	22	57.7[b]	78
Apr 90	18.2	24	57.2[b]	76
May 90	20.2	26	57.3[b]	74
Jun 90	22.4	28	57.0b	72

[a] Convertible-currencies savings were converted to zloty savings at black market rates for 1985-88, at grey market rate for 1989 and the official rate for 1990.
[b] Overstated due to the inclusion of enterprises' convertible-currencies desposits (domestic-currency savings' shares are slightly overstated for respective months of 1990). The share of domestic-currency savings of households was in June 1990 equal to 30.8% of total household savings.

Source: See Tabel 2.1

1990, while the former almost recovered their December 1989 level by the end of June. As a result, the share of domestic currency savings in total savings has been going up all the time (see Table 5).

What interpretation should be given to these developments? First of all, households, just as expected by the permanent income theory, tend to stick to a stable money holdings/incomes ratio (whatever that ratio might be under given, highly unstable circumstances). This happened regardless of interest rates, for negative real interest rates prevailed with respect to 'old' (pre-January 1990) time deposits in the first half of 1990, as can be esaily detected from monthly CPI changes in Table 2.1 and discount rates in Table 2.2. Positive real interest rates for 'new' savings have appeared since March 1990.

An alternative interpretation is also possible, though. Households, facing an uncertain future that includes the probability of being unemployed for the first time since 1939, may have decided to increase precautionary savings ('saving for a rainy day'). Whether the first or the second interpretation is closer to the reality, cannot be established at such an early date. If some stable money holdings/incomes ratio is achieved and maintained while incomes begin to increase again in real terms, then the permanent income hypothesis will receive stronger empirical support.

An important lesson that can be drawn from Polish households' behaviour is that households in post-STEs—if exposed to different economic conditions—change their behaviour accordingly and again behave rationally, i.e., in a way predicted by the relevant theory. This conclusion, if it can be generalized, makes the transition to the market system more predictable and, as such, easier to implement. The impact of experience—of being exposed to changed conditions—is of special importance for the transition. From the late 1950s Poland has been (together with Hungary) a country with relatively high open inflation in comparison with other STEs. This open or officially registered inflation was coupled, as everywhere, with hidden inflation, i.e., price level changes without apparent changes in list prices, and repressed inflation, i.e., shortages and queues. And from the late 1970s it has been an absolutely high open inflation country. Ability to react rationally in the face of high open inflation improved accordingly.

In comparison with Polish households, e.g., Soviet ones are at a disadvantage since their experience has been until very recently one of hidden and repressed inflation only. Since the re-emergence of open inflation is a relatively new phenomenon in the USSR, the money illusion is stronger there. Soviet households' behaviour bears, however, a resemblance to that of Polish households in the late 1970s and during the first 'Solidarity' period (1980/81). The

46

latter's experience with high inflation was then of a recent vintage and their expectations did not yet adapt to the changed conditions. However, other reactions of Soviet households facing accelerating inflation of all types (open, hidden, and repressed) point to a rational adjustment to changing circumstances. Accelerated purchases of durables and—more recently—non-durables have been under way for some time. So has been the change of (some part of) savings into other assets (jewelry, convertible currencies).

The tentative conclusion can be drawn that regardless of decades of indoctrination in Marxist beliefs individuals behave rationally, i.e., as utility maximizing individuals, and adjust their behaviour accordingly in the face of new economic phenomena. A supplementary conclusion would be that the length of exposure to these new phenomena and/or their intensity may also matter.

Behaviour of State-Owned Enterprises

Enterprises everywhere are collectivities and their behaviour—their 'foreign policies' as termed by Wiles (1977)—depends on what is going on inside these collectivities. Moreover, state-owned enterprises (SOEs for short) have property rights assigned in a way that raises transaction costs enormously. Worse still, SOE managers in STEs perform almost without a budget constraint since the government acts as a general insurance agency protecting them against failure (Kornai, 1979; 1980). Furthermore, the symbiotic relationship between politics and economics bred a special type of managers, who are much better in articulate pleading for subsidies or backroom dealing with communist *apparatchiki* than in anything else.

Private enterprises under the pressure of falling traditional demand would seek new markets, cut costs, launch new products, etc. Under the specific post-STE conditions, they would be expected also to look for alternative channels of distribution bypassing state monopsonists in wholesale trade. However, this did not happen. Some adjustment indeed took place. Exports to countries with convertible currencies increased. Some attempts at reaching buyers directly were made (traveling salesmen came back to life here and there). Some, albeit very little, price cutting took place as well. But the option most often chosen was the one least preferred by adjustment theory, that is deep cuts in output accompanied by furloughing (much more rarely laying off) the labour force. (Compare both output and employment decline in Table 2.1.) And there were no bankruptcies, either. Even more surprisingly, most enterprises showed a high profitability in the face of low capacity utilisation rates.

In the author's opinion, the Polish transition programme added to our knowledge of the behaviour of SOE managers. Theorists recognise very well the overexpansionary behaviour of these managers in the Soviet-type economy (see, i.a., Wakar et al. (1965), Bauer et al. (1972), and Kornai (1971; 1980). The same managers who disregarded profitability under the accommodative macroeconomic policy, disregarded it again under the restrictive policy. Regardless of cost, they turned overdeflationary. This symmetry suggests that SOE managers can choose strategies that may run counter to the interest of the owner, i.e., the state, under *any* macroeconomic policy stance. And, let it be added, their *nomenklatura* origins and past STE experience may make them perform at still lower levels of efficiency than that usually displayed by SOE managers elsewhere.

But even this interpretation is offered with great circumspection because the Polish government's policy itself may have contributed importantly to the behaviour in question. SOE managers might have thought—on the basis of past experience with communist governments—that the present government would also reverse its restrictive stance when signs of pain multiplied. Thus, they could play a waiting game and save themselves the strenuous effort to adjust. However, performance indicators should begin over time to show the costs of non-adjustment. But this is not what happened. Most enterprises still continued to show high operating profits. Therefore, other factors have been at work. These 'other factors' are policy mistakes.

Right after the formation of the first non-communist Polish government, its economic team was urged from various quarters (see i.a., Beksiak et al., 1989) to immediately raise the discount rate of the central bank to positive levels in real terms. It was stressed that the period of cheap money and underpriced imports could be ended overnight, without waiting for the 'big bang', and that the continuation of policies inherited from the past would only increase the severity of measures that would have to be taken later to achieve the aims of a reform programme.

Nothing was done, however, with respect to the interest rate and too little—on a piecemeal basis—with respect to the overvalued exchange rate. Enterprises continued to obtain cheap credits and to pay less than the market value for imported raw materials and intermediate products until the very end of 1989. In consequence, they accumulated unusually large input inventories. According to official statistics, while output of state industry fell by 2.5% in 1989, inventories of raw materials and intermediate products increased by 20.9% in the same period (both figures in real terms). Work-in-progress also increased markedly by 15.4%.

The consequences have been obvious: windfall gains resulting from using underpriced inputs (bought at lower prices in 1989) for much higher-priced outputs in 1990 enabled many enterprises to achieve high profits in spite of low sales and capacity utilization rates. Pressure to adjust lessened as a result. The government needed to continue the restrictive monetary policy for some time to eliminate the effects of windfall gains on SOEs behaviour, thus making the transition unnecessarily costly.

Almost everybody tends to stress the restrictive monetary policy since January 1990. Aggregate figures of money supply in real terms in Table 2.2 show that the fall in the real money supply was very sharp in the first two months, but by June the supply was almost at the end-December 1989 level. However, it was the household sector that bore the brunt of monetary stringency. A

Table 2.6

State Enterprises' Deposits in Nominal and Real Terms
(December 1989 = 100)

Month	Deposits (trillion zlotys)	Deposit growth		Wholesale price index[b]
		nominal	real[a]	
Dec 89	7.8	100.0	100.0	100.0
Jan 90	15.2	198.7	94.7	209.8
Feb 90	17.0	217.9	94.2	231.4
Mar 90	19.7	252.6	109.7	230.2
Apr 90	21.7	278.2	119.4	233.0
May 90	27.8	356.4	152.4	233.9
Jun 90	30.5	391.0	163.9	238.5

[a] Denated by the wholesale price index.
[b] Sales' prices of state industrial enterprises.

Source: See Table 2.1

look at Table 2.6, where SOEs' deposits are shown in nominal and real terms, underlines the argument. State enterprises barely felt the stringency in January and February and their money holdings increased fast in real terms after March.

Their relatively good and improving liquidity position was not due to excessive domestic credit expansion. Credits extended to domestic economic agents fell by some 20% in the comparable period in real terms, as seen in Table 2.2. Ample liquidity in most SOEs must have come from different sources. One such source was mentioned already, namely windfall profits from utilising cheaply bought imports. But there was also another source, i.e., the rapid reduction of SOEs' stocks of convertible currencies that they accumulated under the old export incentive scheme. Between January and June 1990 enterprises sold more than $1.7 billion, increasing their domestic money stock considerably. Since the new foreign exchange regime did not allow enterprises to maintain accounts in foreign currencies, the government might have expected that the accumulated stock could be used by SOEs to improve their domestic liquidity position. That it chose to remain passive—or did not even recognise the danger to its monetary policy—was surely a policy mistake.

Whatever the sources, the monetary constraint on SOEs has not been as strong as is generally claimed. And the factors mentioned above undoubtedly contributed to a considerable extent to the rather weak adjustment by SOEs. It is, however, impossible to ascertain to what extent the weak adjustment so far has been a consequence of factors analysed in the first part of this section, that is lack of experience, a special breed of managers and the nature of SOEs themselves, and what was the impact of the government's policy of benign neglect. More time has to pass for short-run factors to disappear and make the picture clearer.

In terms of lessons to be drawn from Polish SOEs' behaviour, there are quite a few even at this stage of development. Certainly those who stressed that not only living under the Soviet economic system but also leaving that system is costly have been right. The capability of the state sector to adjust is rather low. We also learnt that the pressure to adjust may be lessened by policy mistakes of the sort analysed above.

Another adjustment problem of SOEs in post-Soviet-type economies is the problem of dual markets. A substantial part of Polish (and other STEs) exports is directed to COMECON countries with non-convertible currencies, mostly to the USSR. Many exporters, and in the case of engineering industries a large majority of exporters, have enjoyed for years (if not decades) an easy life of exporting to undemanding markets at often quite profitable prices. Their products could hardly be sold outside COMECON without heavy discounts or could not be sold at all.

One might have expected that with the fall of demand for their output in Poland those SOEs would try to increase their exports to the USSR and elsewhere within Eastern Europe even at a low zloty/rouble exchange rate in the hope of obtaining subsidies later on (as happened in the past). In this way, too, they would be able to postpone the adjustment. And this is what happened. In spite of the recession in Soviet industry and similar developments elsewhere in Eastern Europe, Polish SOEs continued their exports to the non-convertible currency area at almost 1989 levels (97.4% of January-June 1989) in the first half of 1990 in real terms. And all this in the face of a 40% fall in imports which made Poland a large scale supplier of interest-free credit to its COMECON partners.

A lesson to be drawn is that in trade with non-market economies market-type measures, such as exchange rates, may not necessarily be effective. This lesson has already been learned by the Yugoslavs and Finns in their trade with the Soviet Union. Although Poland did not at the start avoid the mistake (the government introduced a dual exchange rate system in June 1990, with the new rate for exports being half of the regular rate), others certainly should. The neglect may again have contributed to the weakening of the pressure to adjust.

Government Performance and Short-Run Adjustment

Government monetary, fiscal and exchange rate policies form the basic framework within which forced adjustment is taking place. Worth noting, however, is the fact that in Poland stabilisation measures have been introduced simultaneously with measures to liberalise the economy. This made both government policy more difficult and the performance of the economy less predictable.

It should be said at the outset that the basic thrust of government policy has been right and policy instruments positively correlated to achieve the twin goals of stabilization and liberalization. Thus, monetary policy was considerably tightened on 1 January 1990, although it was a serious error not to do so earlier (as stressed in the preceding section).

The clarity of monetary policy left something to be desired, though. Although the interest rate became clearly the main instrument of the central bank (NBP), credit rationing was also used. Furthermore, commercial banks' credit support for at least some heavy industry giants cannot be explained in terms of the latter's creditworthiness. Thus, the perennial problem of an STE, i.e., a soft budget constraint, has not yet been eliminated.

Fiscal policy was rigorously kept on course, as far as the balanced budget is concerned. The stream of revenue kept pace with the expenditure made, and credits from the central bank were repaid on time and kept within modest limits established by the new budgetary rules. Over time, however, this may (and indeed has) become increasingly difficult. The sources of these difficulties are twofold. On the one hand, a sharp fall in output has reduced the volume of profits, and consequently the corporate income tax volume. On the other hand, the government made—in the author's opinion—a mistake by retaining an asset tax levied on SOEs, misleadingly called 'dividend' by the previous communist government. This little noticed decision may have far-reaching consequences.

Since expansion decisions are taken in STEs by central planners and their political masters, SOEs are often saddled with unviable factories or unfinished investment projects. Financial consequences of these decisions affect even otherwise well-performing enterprises. Thus, the asset tax is affecting SOEs at random. It certainly would have been better to raise corporate income tax from 40% to 50% and to abolish the asset tax altogether.

Since this was not done, the government faces an unpalatable choice. It can either force bankruptcies on those numerous enterprises that are unable to pay for the past profligacy of bureaucrats and *apparatchiki*, or accept the non-payment of the asset tax as a fact of life. And the fact of life is that the asset tax was paid in about two-thirds of the amount expected from the asset-tax time schedule (*Rzeczpospolita*, 30 July 1990). Neither alternative is attractive and both mean that government revenue from asset tax will be very much smaller than planned. Coupled with a smaller expected volume of revenues from corporate income tax, such developments make it difficult to balance the budget—with all their inflationary implications. All the more so, since budget expenditures are rigid and may move only in the upward direction under the conditions of higher than expected inflation and growing unemployment. Another, no less unpalatable, aspect of the asset tax issue is the threat of reemergence of the 'soft' budget constraint in a different guise.

Exchange rate policy should be credited with the right level of devaluation of the zloty at the start of the 'big bang' and blamed for its delay until 1 January 1990 (see the preceding section). Although the zloty was devalued by much less than the actual rate of inflation in January, its dollar rate was then kept stable. Devaluations expected by many did not occur. This was partly a result of the rapid increase in convertible currency reserves due to rising exports and falling imports and partly of the underlying cost/price relationship that continued to be advantageous for export orientation (regardless of domestic demand conditions).

Exchange rate policy or, to be more precise, foreign economic policy, should also be blamed for erecting additional barriers against imports. Fearful of the pressure on the newly established exchange rate, the government decided to introduce customs duties at the 20% level on the average on most goods. And, since the sales tax has also been levied on imports on an *ad valorem* basis (inclusive of customs duties), a large 'wedge' emerged between export and import exchange rates.

Consequences of this overcautiousness on the side of the government were twofold—both adverse. First, the higher import exchange rate raised the price of goods with a high import content and, consequently, reduced domestic demand for these goods, over and above the reduction in demand stemming from restrictive macroeconomic policy. Second, the 'wedge' generally made imports dearer and reduced competitive pressure from imports. Thus, not only could aggregate output have been higher but also prices lower thanks to greater competitive pressure.

Finally, government performance with respect to price and wage controls should be taken into account. Especially wage controls have been a bone of contention. The author understands the preferences of the IMF/World Bank experts who opt for visible 'nominal anchors' that allow them to recognise clearly and unequivocally when a government fails to stick to stabilization targets (it is within this context that the choice of fixed over flexible exchange rate was also made). He will also refrain from the usual free market-type criticism of wage controls.

Two issues, however, require deliberation *within* the context of wage controls. There are two reasons for wage controls under the conditions such as those that existed in Poland in 1989. The first is to shorten the time span of adjustment from hyperinflation to sharply lower rates of change in the price level. The second is to spread the pain of the cut in real wages across all industries.

The particular form of wage controls chosen by the government was a wage bill tax. Any wage increases in excess of a fraction of the price increase allowed by controls (0.3% for every 1% increase in CPI in January and 0.2% in February and March) were penalised by heavy taxes. Even assuming, as the government did, that prices would rise in the first three months by 60-70% not twice as much (as they did), the coefficients would have ensured a fall in real wages by 25-30%.

Such a large fall was presumably necessary to both eliminate forced savings and damp hyperinflationary expectations. However, the government did not take into account the fact that forced savings were to a substantial extent eroded in the last few hyperinflationary months of 1989. Data presented in Table 7 show convincingly how the real value of household savings had fallen quickly between July and December 1989. By the end of December it amounted to only a fraction of what it had been a year before.

The government was clearly too restrictive in its treatment of wages in the light of late 1989 real savings developments. The question, however, to what extent these wage restrictions have influenced the deep fall in output cannot be answered as easily. For it should be noted that most SOEs, facing the fall in demand from their traditional customers, did not even increase wages to the le-

Table 2.7

**Money Holdings of the Household Sector in the
June-December 1989 Period (June 1989 = 100)**

Month	Money holdings (billion zlotys)	CPI	Money holdings nominal	real
Jun	8,737	100.0	100.0	100.0
Jul	9,279	109.4	106.2	97.1
Aug	10,466	152.7	119.8	78.5
Sep	12,005	205.1	137.4	67.0
Oct	13,464	317.3	154.1	48.7
Nov	16,461	388.4	188.4	48.5
Dec	17,529	457.2	200.6	43.9

Source: See Table 2.1

vels allowed under wage controls. It is a widely shared view that restrictive monetary policy with monthly interest rates approaching positive real rates (except for January when they fell far below this level) had the stronger impact on the behaviour of SOEs in this respect.

Thus, wage controls affected output adversely only in those enterprises that enjoyed sufficient demand for their product (in fact it also prevented growth of employment and output in those SOEs that continued to experience growing demand for their products). It is highly speculative but one may wonder to what extent the political legitimacy of the non-communist government contributed to these low wage demands. If pressure for wage increases were higher in the absence of politically motivated restraint in spite of the restrictive macroeconomic framework, then the cost of overly restrictive wage controls would be higher, too.

To some extent the government contributed also to the absence of bankruptcies in the face of the 25-30% fall in output. Other factors were at work here (see the preceding section), but the attempt to spread the cost of real wage decline evenly may also have been influential.

Altogether the government did not avoid mistakes in applying macroeconomic policy instruments. Learning from these mistakes concerns, first of all, monetary and exchange rate policies. All post-STEs entering the period of transition to the market system are in a state of larger or smaller disequilibrium, both internal and external. Therefore, to make the transition period shorter, measures that can be taken on their own, without waiting for the 'big bang', should be introduced as quickly as possible. This applies to both raising the discount rate to positive real level and devaluing the domestic currency to at least the level that eliminates export subsidies.

They should also avoid Polish-type 'prop-ups' to the exchange rate, which are costly in terms of both output losses (due to excessively costly imported inputs) and prices (due to lower import pressure on domestic producers). Post-STEs should note from Polish experience that the exchange rate is a poor instrument in influencing the volume of trade with STEs, and some form of export controls, whenever surpluses are undesirable, may become a necessity. Incidentally, Hungarian policy makers came sooner to that conclusion.

System-Specific Determinants of Output Fall in the Transition Period

It should be noted that the author has carefully refrained so far from asking—let alone answering—the question of whether the fall in output was inevitable in the transition from the Soviet-type economy to a market economy. In the preceding two sections, I stressed only that some legacies of the past and mistaken government policies made output lower than it could have been otherwise. But the 'otherwise' matters, too. If it were not for the foregoing, would output remain at pre-transition level? My answer based on system-specific features of the STE is emphatically in the negative.

There is a share of output in an STE that simply would not have existed in a less wasteful economic system. No less importantly, this output, although it contributes to economic growth of every STE, does not contribute to economic welfare. It is not difficult to find such output with respect to all categories of goods: capital goods, intermediate inputs, and consumer goods. For example, sending enterprise-owned vans and lorries to bring in small quantities of missing parts components, etc., from their suppliers in order to fulfil this or that plan target is a way of life in the STE world where uncertainty of supply reigns supreme and costs of plan fulfillment do not matter. It is for that very reason that every SOE tries to keep as large a fleet of pick-ups, vans and lorries as possible.

Now, with the fundamental realignment of the supply/demand relationship under the restrictive macroeconomic framework (even if often less restrictive than it is generally perceived), suppliers begin to search for purchasers and the old dominant position of the former is disappearing fast. Under such circumstances, suppliers became more disciplined and the time of deliveries is nowadays less of a problem. But this return to normalcy has its consequences. For quite obvious reasons, SOEs will buy less transport equipment than in the past. In the short run, i.e., before transport equipment manufacturers find other markets, output will thus fall.

Capital goods are not the only category of goods where a wasteful economic system generates artificial demand. Intermediates are another category. STE enterprises are noted for their high inventories of inputs (see, e.g., Kornai, 1982; and Winiecki, 1986; 1988). With the changed supply/demand relationship they certainly will adjust their input inventories/output ratios downward. The same happens with consumer goods as well. Food products are the best example. Decades of shortage forced households to make overly large purchases of food products. With the disappearance of shortage, overly large 'precautionary' purchases all but disappeared.

What is most interesting in the foregoing is the fact that the fall of output occurred in all areas of the economy *without* reducing the welfare of the household sector. Also interesting is the fact that almost nobody took that kind of instant quantity adjustment to supply/demand realignment into account even if almost every expert stresses the extreme wastefulness of an STE. (Exceptions are Sirc (1990) and, to the best of my memory, Rostowski, in a conversation with the author.)

A substantial part of the January-February 1990 fall of output was the result of such a quantity adjustment to the changed realities of the supply/demand relationship. But not all. It is well known that waste in an STE is highly concentrated in the enterprise sector. Thus, the largest fall of output should be expected in industries supplying capital and intermediate goods. But this did not happen. The hardest hit were industries supplying mostly consumer goods (see Table 8). Therefore, other determinants of output fall were at work here as well. Policy mistakes affected output adversely through too strong a squeeze on the household sector. This affected adversely the level of consumption and the sales of consumer goods industries.

Thus, the STE economy in transition suffers from the output and welfare loss due to the initial impact of macroeconomic restraint. This is inevitable; otherwise supply/demand realignment would not occur. However, the welfare loss is markedly lower than the output loss because part of the output is system-specific and its disappearance does not reduce welfare. In the case of the Polish transition programme, these output and welfare losses were augmented by policy mistakes.

Therefore, the Polish government (or any other government in such a situation) should resist siren songs of those demanding immediate reflation or at a (slightly) more sophisticated level demanding support for their 'priority' industry or industries, the sum of which makes, not unexpectedly, 'priority' for the economy as a whole (that is, reflation). Unfortunately, the Polish government, battered for wrong reasons by interventionists, seems to be mov-

Table 2.8

Industrial Output by Industry in January- June 1990
(January-June 1989 = 100)

Industry[a]	Output	Industry[a]	Output
Mining	71.9	Building materials	69.2
Coal mining	67.6	Wood, pulp and paper	69.8
Manufacturing	71.2	Wood and wood products	69.4
Metallurgy	82.1	Textiles	57.8
Engineering	76.1	Clothing	63.0
Non-electrical machinery	84.4	Leather and footwear	59.3
Transport equipment	71.2	Food products	62.6
Chemical	73.8	Printing	78.6
Mineral	70.0	Electricity	94.0

[a] Mining, manufacturing and electricity.

Source: See Table 2.1

ing in wrong directions of both mild reflation and some industry-specific measures. The results, coupled with earlier policy mistakes, may not be encouraging for those trying to travel the same road.

One more indirect lesson can be drawn from the foregoing with respect to fiscal policy. If output is expected to fall owing to the short-term adjustment to the change in the supply/demand relation, then cautiousness is advisable with respect to the size of the budget. With output falling, tax receipts should be expected to fall, thus the budget relative to GDP should be made lower *ex ante* than in the pre-transition period. It may turn out to be higher *ex post* when expenditures associated with unemployment grow above planned levels while GDP itself shrinks. But planning a larger budget/GDP ratio before entering the transition period, as the Polish government did, is either dangerous to equilibrium or crowds out the non-budget sector.

From Stabilizing to Higher Effiency: Privatization and Competition Policy in the Transition Programme

The obvious goal of the transition programme is to shift the economy to the higher performance level typical for a market economy. Stabilization is a necessary part (the greater the disequilibrium, the more necessary it is), but certainly not a sufficient one. It is here that the privatization issue comes to the fore. Privatization should be considered in two complementary ways.

First, there is privatization from below, that is creating the environment conducive to the establishment and expansion of private firms. If such firms increase their output, the relative size of the private sector increases *vis-à-vis* that of the state sector. Second, there is privatisation from above, that is the transfer of (a large part of) state sector assets into private hands. This can be achieved in many ways, including outright sales of state enterprises as a whole, sales of some of their assets, sales of shares in enterprises transformed into joint-stock companies, free or token payment-based distribution of assets among employees or citizens, etc.

It is the privatisation understood in the first way that has been most neglected by the government. The private sector not only has to cope with the fall in demand (it coped with it much better than the state sector, anyway, with its output stabilising at the 1989 level in the aggregate after the first 5 months of 1990), but also with the continued nonexistence of the institutional support necessary for normal market-type expansion.

The rate of formation of new firms slowed down but continued to be high. The main problem now is not formation (there are no legal obstacles to speak of), but expansion. Few of them reach the size that would make them efficient subcontractors for larger producers because there are no financial markets to speak of in Poland (or elsewhere in post-STEs), no small-business development banks, no small-business-oriented insurance companies, no financial intermediaries supporting leasing and other deals typical for start-up and small firms, no venture capital institutions or innovation support centres that would encourage innovation by reducing its cost to small firms, etc. The rudimentary banking system is geared to servicing large state enterprises and there is little else by way of financial markets.

Unfortunately, the government concentrated its attention on the privatisation from above and pursued the policy of benign neglect with respect to the private sector. But if there were ever good reasons for using foreign public assistance wisely (with more benefit than damage to the receiving economy), it was in this case. EEC or American assistance could be used to give initial endowments to such private-sector-oriented banks and to pay for private Western expertise to run such institutions in the first few years of their existence. If post-STEs are ever to shift to a normal market economy, they cannot do without the normal organic growth of the private sector. And normal organic growth of the private sector needs an effort in institution-building that cannot be shifted completely onto the shoulders of the fledgling private sector itself. It requires legal, technical and financial assistance from the government and—hopefully—foreign donors willing to assist the transition.

The Polish government so far did nothing in this respect and one of the lessons to be drawn from the Polish programme is that any government that wants the transition to be successful in the longer run should become active in that area as soon as possible. Otherwise, the private sector of Lilliputian firms will continue to be only marginally important for years to come.

As far as privatisation from above is concerned, there are two lessons to be drawn from the experience of the Polish government's work on the privatization bill. The first lesson is to formulate goals of privatisation before its means, that is to do exactly the opposite of what was done in Poland in the October 1989-June 1990 period. The government's leading decision-makers, including those in the Office of the Government Plenipotentiary for Privatization Affairs, were single-mindedly oriented towards the 'classical', British-style sale of shares of privatized enterprises to the general public. Interestingly, it is only after outlining the method (public sale), that the government programme of October 1989 stated somewhat ambiguously that preference would be given to those citizens who buy a small amount of shares. Only indirectly could one surmise that the government's aim was the widest possible dispersion of ownership: a goal known under the more popular name of 'people's capitalism'.

However, for a country only beginning the process of transition back to capitalism, wide dispersion of ownership could be but one of the goals of privatisation. In the United Kingdom, with its plethora of large, medium-sized and small privately-owned firms, dispersion of ownership through public sale enlarged this particular dimension of the existing ownership structure. In Poland or Hungary, where there are only small and a few medium-sized private firms (or in Czecho-Slovakia and other countries of Eastern Europe where there are none), other goals of privatisation are very important.

As stressed by the author elsewhere (Winiecki, 1990b), there is no capitalism without capitalists, that is without those who risk their own capital rather than employment (and some capital on the side). Therefore, any privatization programme in these countries should include measures facilitating the expansion of the capitalist class. It is not enough to wait until the reconcentration of capital takes place through the stock market where shares will be freely sold and bought. Right at the start, small and medium-sized state enterprises employing, say, up to 100, 200 or 250 workers, should be sold as a whole to potential domestic buyers for cash or on a credit basis with, say, a 25% downpayment. (See such suggestions in Beksiak et al. (1989); Winiecki (1990c); and Kornai (1990).)

Leaving aside the narrowness of goals, the choice of privatisation means has also been flawed. The British government privatised about 5% of industrial assets, a dozen or two enterprises, over a period of more than ten years. The Polish government, with more than 90% of industrial assets and about 7,000 industrial enterprises owned by the state, would need a century to complete its task at this rate. And even that assessment does not take into account the striking differences in the level of sophistication and the size of financial markets in the two countries.

Obviously, privatization cannot last a century, or even a few decades. Most enterprises would remain state-owned long after the stabilization programme has been implemented. State enterprises are overexpansionary under accommodative macroeconomic policy. They do not care very much for profitability and they can do it without much risk because the transaction costs in controlling managers of such enterprises are exorbitant. With the overwhelming size of the state sector that means a highly inflationary, disequilibrated economy for decades to come. An alternative, as unpalatable as the foregoing, is to continue restrictive macroeconomic policy for decades. Therefore, privatization has to be speeded up one way or another.

Given the fact that post-STE societies are impoverished and their savings are a very small fraction of the value of privatized assets, credit-supported sale is a minimum that can be done to accelerate privatization for financial reasons. There are, however, near-insurmountable technical obstacles referred to above. Thus, free distribution of shares to either all citizens or employees, or a mixture of both seem to be inevitable if the bulk of state assets is to be privatized within a reasonably short time span, say 5 years.

Better performance in many specific cases cannot be achieved by privatization alone. In a highly concentrated economy, economic agents with better defined property rights are a necessary but not sufficient condition. There are some economic areas where privatisation should be combined with measures breaking the monopoly—at a national or local level—of certain producers of goods and services. To give an example, the average West European construction firm employs typically 20 persons, while the average Polish firm has over 700!

Thus, demonopolization does not mean only subjecting a few national monopolists (such as the tractor producer URSUS) to international competition. It is also a question of specially tailored privatisation programmes for certain industries or even for certain organisations, such as—to give another example—wholesale and retail transport, which is usually in the hands of just one firm for a large city or a region (Warsaw has one such enterprise). A pure and simple privatization would create a strong monopoly facing thousands of small private retailers.

Such special demonopolization measures enhancing competition at the local or national level are particularly important in the case of non-tradeables, i.e., goods and services not traded internationally. The tractor factory, even if it is a monopolist on the domestic market, will come under competitive pressure from foreign firms after the liberalization. On the other hand, local transport or construction firms will not—at least in the short to medium run.

In Place of Conclusions: Is There Only One Sequence of Transition Measures?

The question formulated in the subtitle cannot really be answered on the basis of Polish experience alone. There are, of course, many who, without theoretical or empirical foundations, will argue in favour of some preferred—allegedly costless—alternative transition programme. What I have in mind, however, is not the latest version of the belief in a free lunch but basically two issues: (i) the existence or nonexistence of *the* sequence of stabilization, liberalization and privatization and (ii) possible variations in the degree of restrictiveness of macroeconomic policy. Both, issues are strongly intertwined.

The first issue is whether Poland or any other post-STE had the option of starting demonopolization and privatization first so as to create more competitive structures before liberalizing the economy. In other words, whether it would be able to improve the adjustment capability of the economy and, in consequence, reduce the cost of transition. This seemed to be, e.g., an early preference of the Czecho-Slovak government, but more recent comments of its finance minister are less unambiguous about this option (see Klaus, 1990).

Although a very tentative YES answer seems possible in the writer's view, the range of measures and the time span of preliminary rearrangements made 'from above' before freeing the economy do not seem to be large. Breaking up a number of non-vertically integrated monopolistic state enterprises, making some modest reform of the still state-owned banking system as a first step to the restoration of financial markets, and establishing a legal framework for privatization, may be a few more steps. Other decisions have to be made via the market or at the very least have to be verified by the market. And this can be done only when the market comes into being, i.e., after liberalization.

Thus, establishing more competitive structures before liberalizing the economy is only possible to a limited extent, and those few demonopolizing and privatizing measures can precede liberalization by a rather short period of time. And the larger the disequilibrium at the beginning of the transition programme, the shorter that period can be, approaching zero in the case of severe disequilibrium of the hyperinflationary type.

For that reason the Polish government did not have an opportunity at the end of 1989 to choose a sequence of liberalizing and privatizing measures according to its preference, but had to start with liberalization as a concomitant to stabilization (if it wanted to avoid 'more of the same', that is attempting stabilization by government fiat only). On the other hand, Czecho-Slovakia, with its least disequilibrated economy among STEs, was quite clearly in a different, more advantageous situation. As can easily be seen, this has nothing to do with the quality of the Czechoslovak transition programme per se but is the consequence of the initial macroeconomic conditions in that country as compared to that of Poland (or the USSR for that matter).

Altogether there is no one and only sequence of transition measures. But alternatives seem to be limited in both time and scope, and the very existence of choice depends on macroeconomic conditions in the country undergoing transition. In extremely disequilibrated, inflationary conditions, the choice of the sequence approaches zero, which means that costs of the transition cannot be reduced on that basis alone.

The choice of the degree of macroeconomic restriction seems to be even narrower. After all, restrictive monetary and fiscal policies are needed to alter the long-lasting supply/demand relation, as well as a response to the degree of excess demand existing in the economy at the start of the transition. The share which restrictive macroeconomic measures equilibrating the economy account for in the total costs of transition depends clearly on the degree of excess demand existing at the start of a transition programme.

References

Bauer, R., Beksiak, J. et al. (1972), *Political Economy of Socialism*, Warsaw, in Polish.

Beksiak, J., Gruszecki, T., Jedraszczyk, A. & Winiecki, J. (1989), *Outline of a Programme for Stabilisation and Systemic Changes*, Warsaw, September, mimeo. English version, see (1990), *The Polish Transformation: Programme and Progress*, Centre for Research into Communist Economies, London, July.

Blue Ribbon Commission: Project Hungary (1990), *Action Programme for Hungary in Transformation to Freedom and Prosperity*, Budapest, April, mimeo.

Grossman, G. (1963), 'Notes for a Theory of the Command Economy', *Soviet Studies*, Vol. 15.

Klaus, V. (1990), 'Political and Economic Reform in Eastern Europe: A Case of Czechoslovakia'. A paper prepared for The Mont Pelerin Society General Meeting: 'Europe in an Open World Order', Munich, 2-8 September, mimeo.

Kornai, J. (1971), *Anti-Equilibrium: On Economic Systems Theory and the Tasks of Research*, Amsterdam.

Kornai, J. (1979), 'Resource-Constrained versus Demand-Constrained Systems', *Econometrica*, Vol. 47.

Kornai, J. (1980), *Economics of Shortage*, Amsterdam.

Kornai, J. (1982), *Growth, Shortage and Efficiency: A Macroeconomic Model of the Socialist Economy*, Oxford.

Kornai, J. (1990), *The Road to a Free Economy: Shifting from a Socialist System: The Example of Hungary*, New York.

Sirc, L. (1990), 'Markets Spell Disaster?', Introduction to *The Polish Transformation: Programme and Progress*, Centre for Research into Communist Economies, London, July.

Wakar, A., ed. (1965), *Outline of Theory of Socialist Economy*, 2nd edition. Warsaw, in Polish.

Wiles, P.J.D. (1977), *Economic Institutions Compared*, Oxford.

Winiecki, E.D. & Winiecki, J. (1987), 'Looking at Quantity Only Rather than Quantity cum Quality', Warsaw, mimeo.

Winiecki, E.D. & Winiecki, J. (1990), 'Quality Differences in American-Soviet Consumption Comparisons: Comparing the Soviet and American Economies', Conference paper, American Enterprise Institute for Public Policy Research, Washington, D.C., April 19-22.

Winiecki, J. (1982), 'Investment Cycles and an Excess Demand Inflation in Planned Economies: Sources and Processes', *Acta Oeconomica*, Vol. 28.

Winiecki, J. (1986), 'Distorted Macroeconomics of Central Planning: An Approach to Theory and Evidence', *Banca Nazionale del Lavoro Quarterly Review*, Vol. 157.

Winiecki, J. (1987), 'Why Economic Reforms Fail in the Soviet System. A Property Rights-Based Approach', Seminar Paper No. 374, Institute for International Economic Studies, Stockholm, mimeo.

Winiecki, J. (1988), *The Distorted World of Soviet-Type Economies*, London.

Winiecki, J. (1990a), *Resistance to Change in the Soviet Economic System: A Property Rights Approach*, London.

Winiecki, J. (1990b), 'Converting Command Economies: No Capitalism Minus Capitalists', *Financial Times*, 20 June.

Winiecki, J. (1990c), 'Privatization in Soviet-Type Economies: Some Crucial Differences and Problems', *Economic Affairs*, Vol. 10.

3 Poland: Micro complications and policy errors or what went wrong?

When the present writer assessed the Polish transition programme at mid-1990 (Winiecki, 1990a), the assessment was on balance highly positive with respect to stabilisation. Near hyperinflation had disappeared (and this in spite of far reaching price liberalisation), the large budget deficit had disappeared as well and there was a fast growing surplus on foreign trade. The price paid for this was a sharp fall in output and rising unemployment, although at a much slower rate.

I pointed out, however, that a large part of that output was in fact system-specific waste that disappeared at the early stage of the transition to the market. Its disappearance signified in reality the decline in the use of inputs per unit of output, i.e. economic gain through higher efficiency, rather than economic loss (see Winiecki, 1990a; 1990b; 1991d). Thus, real costs were lower than statistical ones.

A year later the transition, and even its stabilisation part, was assessed in strikingly different terms. At one end of the spectrum, especially within the country, it was seen as an unmitigated disaster, at the other, optimists, who were few and far between, saw nothing wrong with the stabilization programme as such and ascribed the mounting problems only to deterioration in the external environment. This was the view of the Polish government's macroeconomic team, of international institutions and some Western experts and journalists (apart from the government's pronouncements—see, e.g., report of a meeting with a high-ranking IMF official, Mr Richard Erb, *Zycie Gospodarcze*, 1991, No. 20; Gomulka, 1991; Martin Wolf, *Financial Times*, 3 May 1991; *Business Week*, Special Report, 11 April 1991).

This author is situated somewhere in the middle. He regards the stabilisation programme as by and large sound in its principles but on the verge of an extremely costly failure. This looming failure is the product of accumulating effects of policy errors and transplantation of policy instruments without regard for the different institutional environment of the post-Soviet-type economy in which these instruments have to operate. Application of these policy instruments often brings about perverse effects. As things get worse rather than better, the whole programme comes under threat.

Mid-1990 to Mid-1991: On a Keynesian Roller-coaster

The basically positive assessment at mid-1990 could not, or at the very least should not, have allowed us to ignore some worrying and/or puzzling aspects of the situation. First, inflation did not disappear but stabilised after March 1990 within a 3-5% per month range. This in itself was not unusual: post-hyperinflation recovery has often been accompanied by 'inertial' inflation (see, e.g., Dornbusch, Sturzenegger, Wolf, 1990; and Bernholz, 1990). However, over the next year it did not decline. In the second quarter of 1991 it was about the same as it was in the second quarter of 1990.

More worryingly, inflation continued in spite of the surprisingly large budget surplus at mid-1990, as well as the steep fall in real wages. The traditional inflation-boosting phenomena were thus absent in mid-1990. Next, output recovery was not forthcoming and this was definitely more puzzling. Although part of the output fall could be seen as an adjustment to a more efficient economic system, recovery was barely noticeable in the second quarter of 1990. Furthermore, nobody expected a fall of such magnitude (whether adjustment to a more efficient system was taken into account or not).

Last but not least, the steep fall in real wages (even if overstated by statistics) should have been expected to give rise to wage claims aimed at recovering a part of the lost purchasing power. Wage controls implied that these claims would politicise the wage conflict since they shifted claims from enterprise to government level.

Under such circumstances some macroeconomic policy change had to be expected, accompanied by other measures correcting effects of the STE legacy on the transition process. The latter measures were all the more necessary as state-owned enterprises (SOEs) were not adjusting to the new conditions as rapidly as expected. In some respects adjustment was not only slow but also perverse. This happened in spite of the perceived restrictive macroeconomic policy framework—this was at least a near-consensus view (see, however, Winiecki, 1990a).

Not unexpectedly, then, the summer of 1990 brought some macroeconomic policy change. The central bank (NBP) reduced the interest rate further (and shifted it from a monthly to an annual basis) to 34% per annum for refinancing loans for commercial banks (the central bank's basic lending rate). This amounted to a decrease from 4% to 2.5% on a monthly basis, probably too large a decrease for a modest stimulation, considering the monthly inflation rate in the second quarter.

Fiscal policy was slightly less restrictive but in a wrong way. Deferment of tax payments was agreed when applied for, and 're-interpretation' of indexation rules created greater room for wage increases too. Gradual reduction of the budget surplus and elimination of wage controls would in my opinion have been a sounder way of reducing the degree of macroeconomic restraint.

The foregoing had some macroeconomic effects. Industrial output, that stagnated from March until May, picked up in June

(4.9% on a month-to-month basis) and continued by and large un-interrupted till September 1990 at a rather rapid pace, a 12.2% dip in the holiday month of July notwithstanding. However, output was again flat in October. The price pattern did not change, though. Inflation continued within a 3-5% per month range. The best month was certainly August 1990, when industrial output grew by 7.6% over the preceding month (albeit after the traditional July output dip), while the consumer price index (CPI) increased by 1.8% only. This abatement of inflation turned out to be only a one-month departure from the range observed since March, though, and the CPI growth rate moved back to its earlier range (4.6% in September).

This obviously unnerved the government macroeconomic team and influenced the central bank, which increased its basic lending rate from 34% to 43% on an annual basis in October (3% per month), which might have been closer to the rate needed in the face of continuing inflation at 3-5% per month. The October inflation rate did not show any decline and the central bank raised its basic rate again in November to 55% (3.7% per month). This overhasty, nervous reaction to monthly changes in basic indicators that might have been influenced by random or seasonal phenomena had momentous consequences. After October 1990 output was strongly influenced by the rising cost of money. Output and inflation data are shown in Table 3.1.

It is, of course, possible that the government had hoped for a continuing quarter by quarter decline in inflation and took the August CPI growth rate as supporting its expectations and the September price jump not as a return to an underlying rate but as a signal of renewed inflationary pressures. Policy-makers acted, however, without much reflection on the real meaning of a one-month dip, which did not justify such far-reaching conclusions. (Actually, they acted also without much regard for the easily predictable consequences of the deteriorating external environment of the Polish economy and the interaction of sharp interest rate in-

Table 3.1

Industrial Output and CPI Changes, July 1990–June 1991
(on Monthly Basis: Preceding Month = 100[a])

Month	Output	CPI
July 1990	87.8	103.6
August 1990	107.6	101.8
September 1990	108.0	104.6
October 1990	100.4	105.7
November 1990	100.0	104.9
December 1990	103.2	105.9
January 1991	82.4	112.7
February 1991	100.8	106.7
March 1991	100.1	104.5
April 1991	91.7	102.7
May 1991	98.3	102.7
June 1991	98.3	102.7

[a] ID comparable time.

Sources: Biuletyn Statystyczy GUS (monthly):
Informacja o Sytuacji Spoleczno Gospodarczej Kraju.
GUS (monthly): Informacja o Sytuacji Gospodarczej.
CUP (monthly & quarterly).

creases with these consequences—see the section on 'autonomous' policy errors).

Monetary policy was thus loosened in summer 1990 and then tightened sharply in October and November. Fiscal policy, in turn, continued its restrictive stance for most of the year and only in the last month did the government try feverishly to reduce the budget surplus (quite probably fueling inflation in this way, as the speed of change is an important factor in creating inflationary pressure). Changes in the budgetary balance are shown in Table 3.2. All these shifts were accompanied by firm declarations of an unchanged macroeconomic policy course.

The inflation rate continued within the 3-5% per month range throughout the rest of 1990 (see Table 3.1) and this was seen as a revival of inflationary pressures although there was no difference between the second and fourth quarter and very little difference

Table 3.2

State Budget Balance, January 1990–June 1991
(Cumulative, in Billion Zlotys)[a]

Month	Budget Balance	Month	Budget Balance
January 1990	0.9	January 1991	0.9
February 1990	1.6	February 1991	- 0.7
Msrch 1990	1.8	March 1991	- 6.2
April 1990	5.1	April 1991	- 9.8
May 1990	7.2	May 1991	- 9.6[b]
June 1990	6.5		
July 1990	8.4		
August 1990	9.2		
Septcmber 1990	8.7		
October 1990	9.9		
November 1990	8.8		
December 1990	2.4		

Note: minus sign means deficit.

[a] State budget, including budgets of local administrations.
[b] Postponed expenditure and unpaid bills amounted in May to approximately 30 billion zlotys.

Sources: as Table 3.1

between the third and fourth quarter (whatever difference there was stemmed from the one-month dip in August). Nonetheless, the macroeconomic team took all this very seriously and designed a policy package for 1991 that was far more restrictive than envisaged a few months earlier.

Apart from a sharply higher interest rate raised still further in January 1991), the package attempted to reduce the level of budgetary expenditure in real terms in 1991 and tightened wage controls. It is not certain what role was envisaged in this package for the exchange rate. Fixed in January 1990—originally for three months—it continued to be fixed *vis-à-vis* the US$ throughout the year and policy makers showed no intention to change it in any way. Whether it was seen as an instrument of pressure on SOEs to adjust under competitive pressures from abroad or as a part of the anti-inflationary package for 1991 is a mystery for the present writer. Whatever the intention, the effects were perverse.

Another mystery for the present writer is the government's growth projection for 1991, prepared at about the same time (autumn 1990). GDP growth of 4% per annum in 1991 was under the circumstances completely unrealistic. Growing demand for goods and services has to come from somewhere. However, no demand component looked promising for 1991, given the policy package prepared and, let us add, the external environment of the Polish economy.

Private consumption was to remain restrained since the government planned more restrictive wage controls for the state sector (still more than three-quarters of employment). The abolition of wage controls in the private sector was of limited help in this respect. Public consumption was not expected to give an additional stimulus as an attempt was made to reduce the level of budget expenditure in real terms. Investment was not very likely to give much boost to economic growth, either, after the sharp rise in interest rates, even though the government projected 20% growth of investment in real terms for 1991 (sic).

Last but certainly not least, foreign demand did not look promising at all. A sharp rise in oil prices accentuated the cyclical slow-down in the West, reducing export prospects in this direction. The loss of Iraqi and Kuwaiti markets was also significant. Worst of all, the change to convertible currency trade with the USSR and other ex-COMECON countries was widely expected to lead to a steep fall in exports (many expected Eastbound exports to be cut by half).

On top of exogenous factors reducing demand for Polish exports, the exchange rate policy of the central bank weakened these prospects even further as the exchange rate was maintained throughout 1990 in the face of a CPI increase of 249.3% (and a quasi-WPI increase of 191.5%) from December 1989 to December 1990. Although the devaluation at the end of December 1989 was substantial enough to compensate for expected price increases after liberalisation in January 1990, it was not sufficient to compensate for a 60% loss of purchasing power of the US$ *vis-à-vis* the zloty by the end of 1990.

There were thus no components of final demand that warranted the optimism displayed by the government's macroeconomic team. Even the expected buoyancy of the private sector was under threat of being throttled by very high interest rates. The optimism of the team went beyond growth projections and extended to the budget too, often on the basis of unrealistic expectations about budgetary receipts.

Reality usually differs from carefully (and even more so from carelessly) designed programmes. The election of Walesa to the presidency resulted in a government shake-up. The macroeconomic team remained in place, however, in order to signal to foreign creditors and international institutions the willingness of the new government to continue the transition programme, with all its fundamental features. Nonetheless, some corrections had to be made to fulfil at least some of the promises made during the presidential campaign.

Budget expenditure increased and so did receipts (albeit to a much lesser extent). A small deficit was projected but even this did not satisfy various government critics. As a result, the budget was not formally accepted by parliament until well into 1991. Given the government's optimism with respect to receipts, a substantially larger deficit might have been expected.

Expansion of budget expenditure apart, all other demand components suggested stagnation if not actual contraction of output in 1991. This is what the present writer warned about in a letter to the presidential chancery in December 1990, later circulated privately in mimeo form (Winiecki, 1990c). Macroeconomic developments in the first half of 1991 proved me right. Industrial output stagnated after October 1990 (a small rise in December, a month usually characterised by much larger output increases everywhere, does not contradict this view) and then slid precipitously by 17.6% in January 1991, with further declines in March-May.

Thus, Poland became the only one among the post-Soviet-type economies to undergo a second (in this author's view policy- induced) recession. In Hungary and Czecho-Slovakia the primary, corrective recession continued for the third and second year respectively, as these countries opted for less drastic stabilisation packages. In Poland the primary corrective recession that was expected to change the demand/supply relationship and wring out hyperinflation was sharper but ended earlier. Output started inching upward from June 1990. It stagnated, however, toward the end of 1990 and began declining again from January 1991 under the impact of the sharp increase in the central bank's basic lending rate (increased again in January 1991 to 72% on an annual and 4.6% on a monthly basis) combined with bank-by-bank credit rationing. Thus the seeds of recession were already visible in the autumn of 1990 before the impact of the drastic fall in exports to the USSR and other ex-COMECON countries began to be felt. That is why I call it a policy-induced recession. Within the framework of this policy the moderate correction of the interest rate and exchange rate in May 1991 was seen by many as too little too late.

Inflation continued within a 3-5% range, with outliers scattered here and there (the highest, in January 1991, reflected large increases in regulated energy prices, and there was a low figure in April 1991). This suggests the existence of an underlying inflation rate almost independent of the level of interest rates and the exchange rate, that is, of the cost of money and of competitive pressures. Attempts to throttle this type of inflation through orthodox monetary and other macroeconomic measures were evidently unsuccessful.

This suggests that other measures are also needed to achieve this end. Nonetheless, the government's macroeconomic team, supported by other mostly foreign experts (who did not have any earlier experience with the Soviet-type economy and its possible impact upon transition) persisted in the conviction that they were on the right course. However, the perverse effects of such policies were clear to some other members of the government. For example, the Minister for Industry stressed that the best enterprises were on the verge of bankruptcy, while the worst ones were surviving without much effort (*Zycie Gospodarcze*, 1991, No. 18).

By the end of January 1991 more than 500 SOEs had lost creditworthiness (the number almost doubled subsequently), yet no bank-initiated bankruptcy proceedings against SOEs to recover debts took place. Nor were they initiated by one SOE against another. Quite obviously, the microeconomic sphere of state-owned banks and state-owned industrial enterprises behaved differently than expected. It is also significant that there were no large enterprises among the SOEs which lost their creditworthiness. Since large enterprises have historically been least efficient under the Soviet economic system, this phenomenon suggests that other forces were at work than the selection mechanism through a macroeconomic restraint assumed to eliminate the least efficient producers.

Thus, relatively better (rather than worse) SOEs came increasingly under the threat of bankruptcy. In a parallel development SOEs have been increasingly in arrears with respect to taxes. By the end of April 1991 2700 SOEs owed 9.8 billion zlotys in unpaid taxes, i.e. one-third more than the budget deficit at that time. Again, arrears did not decline after April. Thus, yet another success of mid-1990 came under threat—the balanced budget (in mid-May 1991 the Central Planning Board did not exclude the possibility of the deficit reaching 26 billion zlotys, that is 3-4% of the projected GDP (*Gazeta Bankowa*, 1991, No. 21)). Little was left of the highly positive tone of the mid-1990 assessment: what went wrong?

Microeconomic Foundations of Macroeconomic Failure

The failure has its roots in the interaction between the microeconomic and macroeconomic spheres, the outcome of which belies the expectations of policy-makers (and their advisers) about the behaviour of economic agents under policies pursued through orthodox 'Keynesian' measures: manipulation of interest rates, taxes and the budget, while maintaining a fixed exchange rate and, in addition, strict wage controls.

In the atypical world of post-Soviet-type economies, as in Poland, these measures do not necesssarily yield the results expected under the market system with dominant private ownership. In this respect, post-STEs with their near exclusive non-private ownership—especially among larger firms—differ not only from well functioning market economies of the West but also from distorted market economies of Asia or Latin America (see Winiecki, 1991b).

Macro-to-micro: Insufficient Pressure on SOEs to Adjust Throughout 1990

Private enterpises facing falling demand generally try to cut costs, launch new products, seek new channels of distribution, new markets, etc. SOEs in the post-STE, however, have property rights assigned in a way that enormously increases transaction costs, as there is almost no owners' control over the management. Adjustment to falling demand may be quite different under these circumstances.

There has been almost universal agreement that SOEs did not adjust sufficiently rapidly and, moreover, in some respects their adjustment has been perverse. Although some adjustment did take place (reduction of inventories, search for alternative distribution channels domestically and, significantly, shift of a larger share of output to foreign markets), the dominant response has been passive adjustment through reduction in output combined with furloughing (more rarely laying off) the labour force. Attempts at

Table 3.3

Household and SOE Deposits in National Currency, July 1990–June 1991, in Nominal and Real Terms

Month	Houschold deposits			SOE deposits		
	In billion zlotys	Nominal change December	Real change 1989 = 100a	In billion zlotys	Nominal change December	Real change 1989 = 100[a]
July 1990	52.3	299	107	38.9	442	179
Aug 1990	56.6	323	113	46.3	526	204
Sept 1990	61.9	354	119	48.5	551	187
Oct 1990	66.2	378	120	51.6	586	190
Nov 1990	71.0	406	123	54.5	637	200
Dec 1990	77.5	443	127	51.8	589	178
Jan 1991	76.5	437	111	55.4	629	174
Feb 1991	87.4	499	119	54.0	614	157
March 1991	96.4	551	126	55.8	634	164
April 1991	106.4	608	134	60.5	687	176
May 1991				61.6	700	176

[a] Deflated by CPI.
[b] Deflated by quasi-WPI.
[c] First month in which bousehold deposits exceeded the already very low December 1989 level.

Sources: as Table 3.1

raising prices were also more numerous than those aimed at cost cutting.

However, one important issue has not really been explored, namely, to what extent were SOEs forced to adjust. The present writer already stressed the point earlier (Winiecki, 1990a) insisting that SOEs were not under strong pressure in the first half of 1990, i.e. the period that, with both high nominal (and later also real) interest rates and deep cuts in subsidies, has been widely regarded as one of severe restriction. He pointed out that although households were severely squeezed, SOEs—in contrast—were not. Table 3.3 supports this contention. Fast growth of SOEs' deposits in real terms suggests a relatively good and improving liquidity position throughout the period.

This good position did not result from credit expansion (credits to domestic economic agents fell between December 1989 and June 1990 by some 20% in real terms). But SOEs found other sources of financial support to survive the macroeconornic squeeze. First, their input inventories (generally much larger relative to output than those in Western enterprises) increased still further in 1989 as near-hyperinflation created additional incentives in this respect. In consequence, input inventories in industry increased by 20% (!), with the purchases fuelled by ever cheaper money (as interest rates were not raised anywhere near positive real levels in the face of fast price increases). The same applied to imported inputs (since the exchange rate was not devalued sufficiently to make up for very much faster domestic price increases). Altogether cheaply bought inputs used in highly priced outputs after price liberalisation in January 1990 ensured high profitability even at low-capacity utilisation rates.

There was yet another source of liquidity, namely the stock of convertible currencies accumulated by enterprises under the export retention scheme (ROD). Since the right of enterprises to keep foreign exchange accounts was abolished under the transition programme, SOEs drew down this stock rapidly, reducing it by 60% between December 1989 and June 1990 (i.e. by US$1.7 billion). Although these consequences of the change in foreign exchange regime were not difficult to predict, no attempt was made by the government to neutralise at least a part of the expected money inflow.

Lastly, as the shift to exports gathered pace, while imports were trailing behind, the trade surplus became another, more lasting source of liquidity for exporting enterprises. Whatever the sources, monetary constraint on SOEs in the January-June 1990 period was not as strong as is generally claimed. What is worth emphasising here, though, is that tightening macroeconomic policy required other measures as well as interest rate increases (such as neutralisation of the domestic currency effects of abolishing foreign exchange accounts).

Table 3.4

Central Bank's Basic Lending Rate, July 1990–June 1991
(on Monthly and Annual Basis)

Month	Monthly rate	Annual rate
July 1990	2.8	34
August 1990	2.8	34
September 1990	2.8	34
October 1990	3.6	39
November 1990	4.6	47
December 1990	4.6	55
January 1991	4.6	55
February 1991	6.0	72
March 1991	6.0	72
April 1991	6.0	72
May 1991	4.8	59

Source: Biuletyn Statystyczny GUS (monthly); Narodowy Bank Polski: I Kwartal—Ocena Wstepna (quarterly).

One could have expected that later in the year, as stocks of cheaply bought inputs and accumulated convertible currencies declined markedly, the degree of pressure to adjust would increase. As stressed in the preceding section, however, interest rates were reduced and credit expansion accelerated in summer 1990 (see Table 3.4). The pressure to adjust decreased in fact. Consequently, macroeconomic policy influenced microeconomic adjustment of the state enterprise sector the wrong way.

Micro-to-micro: Interaction of 'Nobody's' Banks and 'Nobody's' Industrial Firms

Under normal, 'textbook' conditions there is no other way of wringing out inflation from the economy than gradual or sharp tightening of monetary policy (Keynesians who advise Polish policy makers add also wage controls). However, under the far from normal conditions of a post-STE, manipulation of interest rates may be a necessary but not a sufficient condition to achieve this goal. What is missing among policy makers and their advisers is the realisation that state-owned banks and state-owned industrial firms do not behave the way their private counterparts do in the market economy.

Since costs of control are extremely high in the case of an abstract owner, i.e. the state (see, *inter alia*, Furubotn & Pejovich, 1972; Jensen & Meckling, 1976; Demsetz, 1980), state-owned commercial banks do not look at their clients the way privately owned banks do in the West. Historically, they have always been lending first of all to large SOEs and—partly prodded by inertia—they continue to do so under the changed regime.

Banks owned by 'nobody' are run by bureaucrats who rarely know what prudent lending policy is about and even if they do they rarely care. The creditworthiness of their clients is not a matter of serious concern to them. Although, at the request of the central bank, they compile a list of enterprises that have lost creditworthiness, they do not draw conclusions from the fact. A study by the central bank (see *Informacja NBP*, 1991) reveals that by the end of January 1991 there had been no case where a commercial bank initiated bankruptcy proceedings against a debtor. About half of the enterprises concerned were on the list of uncreditworthy ones for about half a year, yet no bankruptcy took place. Obviously, either these enterprises could do without credit or they obtained it regardless of their lack of creditworthiness.

Lending inertia is matched by borrowing inertia. 'Nobody's' enterprises are not concerned to the same extent as private enterprises by a balooning debt-to-equity ratio. In fact, a question posed that way would be greeted in many SOEs with incomprehension: they are unaccustomed to think in those terms. As long as there is money to pay wages, things do not look too bad: and many SOEs borrow exactly for that purpose. Trade unions, self-management bodies and employees are all steeped in the past and many still think that somebody owes workers an undemanding work pace and low but secure wages. There are no owners ready to intervene, shake up the management and try to save the firm. Nobody speaks in the name of capital. The ghost of bankruptcy is still for most enterprises precisely that—a ghost. When things get really bad and a consensus emerges that something should be done it is usually too late.

It is not only inertia that carries over the old pattern of behaviour: so does the political economy of transition. Old *nomenklatura* linkages that generated the 'soft' budget constraint under the STE regime still exist here and there but, worse still, new political linkages affect monetary policy in the same manner. Linkages between enterprise managers, communist party apparatus and banks or ministries (see, *inter alia*, Winiecki 1989 and 1991a) have been largely superseded by those between self- management bodies and 'Solidarity' enterprise-level union organisations, 'Solidarity' regional federations and friendly local officials and parliamentarians who try to influence banks and ministries to come to the rescue. Since state banks' managers are still *de facto* appointed by bureaucrats, not by private shareholders, they are sensitive to outside pressure. In this manner the 'soft' budget constraint has been resurrected in the transition process.

There is, just as in the not-so-distant past, a very specific pattern of leniency in lending. It is the biggest SOEs, possessing the strongest political clout, that encounter no problems in borrowing. As we have seen, the list of 523 enterprises that had lost their creditworthiness by the end of January 1991 included no large enterprises; they were all still regarded as creditworthy, evidently. In a paradoxical way they are, because they believe that if the worst comes to the worst the state will bail them out. This assumption was even articulated *expressis verbis* by a left-leaning 'Solidarity' leader, Bujak, who said that Ursus, the large tractor-producing enterprise, was too big a firm simply to go bankrupt (quoted in *Gazeta Wyborcza*, 19 February 1991). Many do not say so but act on the basis of the same premise. No level of interest rate is high enough to deter them from borrowing. The consequences of such a pattern of behaviour by state-owned banks and enterprises are highly damaging for the economy in transition to the market.

Micro-to-micro: Perverse effects of Interest Rate Manipulation under Different Ownership Structure

Monetary policy in Poland since January 1990 has been pursued mainly through the manipulation of interest rates (plus changes in reserve ratio and, less fashionably, credit ceilings for individual large, state-owned commercial banks). However, the interest rate is not a very efficient anti-inflationary or, conversely, stimulatory measure where the ownership structure differs radically from that of a capitalist market economy. Five quarters (from the second quarter of 1990 to the second quarter of 1991) of persistent inflation at a basically unchanged monthly rate ranging between 3% and 5% should be regarded as sufficiently convincing evidence of this.

In reality, the impact of interest rate manipulation on persistent inflation not only weak but to a large extent perverse, i.e. its outcomes are the opposite of those intended by policy makers. The assumption behind restrictive monetary policy is that higher cost of money will lead to positive natural selection of enterprises and projects, with those more profitable expanding or surviving, while the less profitable contract or leave the market. In the light of what I have said above, this assumption is clearly wrong for a post-Soviet-type economy such as Poland. Let us outline the sequence of events under monetary policy applied in the manner described above. In reality, it will be a re-run of Poland's monetary policy between September 1990 and May 1991.

Policy makers interpret a rise in the monthly inflation rate not as a variation within a range displayed in the recent past but as an upward shift. The Keynesian reaction is to raise interest rates. Impatience, coupled with belief in quick results of such manipulation, makes them repeat the move again if the inflation rate does not decline almost instantaneously. Thus, in Poland the central bank's basic lending rate was raised twice—from 34% to 43% and later to 54%—within two months. The credit squeeze begins to bite. But does it bite whom it should? The answer is no. Inertial lending plus political clout result in a situation where the largest and generally least efficient SOEs will generally obtain the credit they ask for anyway. But other, smaller and relatively more efficient SOEs will get less. Firstly, they borrow somewhat more prudently and are often deterred by very high interest rates. Secondly, if there are credit ceilings on a per bank basis, the shrinking credit total affects them first. Thus, it is the relatively better SOEs that are adversely affected by interest rate increases. As they face mounting difficulties and sometimes totter on the edge of bankruptcy, the output structure deteriorates rather than improves. Private enterprises are also adversely affected. Although a share of credits set aside for the private sector protects them against being crowded out, nothing protects them against the high price they have to pay for borrowed money. Since few projects can be so profitable, output expansion slows down or even declines in the private sector as well. Output structure in the whole economy becomes even worse (quite apart from the stagnating output level).

Inflation, however, continues within the same range as before (see Table 3.1). This is not surprising for the present writer. Large SOEs, immune to the threat of bankruptcy, will continue to raise prices. Some of them enjoy a monopolistic position unaffected as yet by external competition, others are not much afraid of the fall in demand resulting from a price increase (after all, the shortfall in cash flow will be made up by new credits ...).

Without more competition, changes in the ownership structure and attempts at hardening the 'soft' budget constraint, there will be little improvement. Yet this is not the philosophy of the Polish government's macroeconomic team, its advisers or—let us add—the IMF in the background. Their reaction usually 'more of the same'. Inflation continues (in Poland it increased, as the government raised controlled energy prices in January 1991, and policy makers decided to raise interest rates again to 72% on an annual basis). The results? Adverse selection of borrowers continues. Output structure worsens still more. Economic activity is even more severely hit. A push turns into a shove. Stagnation turns into decline.

This is the picture of the Polish economy between September 1990 and May 1991. The outcome is continuing inflation and a shrinking economy. Within the shrinking economy the output share of the worst performers increase rather than decreases. These results are exactly the opposite of those expected under textbook conditions with a different ownership structure.

One may ask whether the opposite direction of monetary policy would bring about as perverse results as monetary restriction. On theoretical grounds one may expect somewhat less adverse effects. Assuming that the volume of credit for those large SOEs with strong political clout is by and large fixed (in real terms), relaxation of monetary policy would be expected to increase the volume of credit for relatively more efficient smaller SOEs and for private firms, thanks to low interest rates and (where applicable) higher credit ceilings. Output would increase and its structure improve to some extent.

This is in practice what happened in Poland in summer 1990. As the level of economic activity began inching upward after the sharp fall in January-February 1990, stimulative monetary policy (may be too stimulative—see the preceding section) raised the output growth rate. Industrial output increased in August and September by an impressive 7.6% and 8% on a month-to-month basis. No doubt, a part of it was an increase in output by protected large monopolists; but in tandem with this adverse outcome better performers increased their output rate too—and their share in total output. Not only did the level of output rise (a normal consequence of macroeconomic stimulation) but the output structure improved too. Inflation, however, continued as it did under more restrictive policy. Obvious recommendations here seem to be less hasty manipulation of interest rates, smoother changes (if necessary) and, most importantly, application of some specific measures addressing the problem of linkages between 'nobody's' banks and 'nobody's' enterprises.

For quite apart from the critical view of overhasty reactions to short-run changes in the inflation rate, a more fundamental critique needs to be directed at the government's philosophy of monetary policy. Throughout the period under consideration there has been little understanding of the increasingly obvious fact that orthodox monetary measures, such as manipulation of interest rates, may be necessary but not sufficient to cope with persistent inflation under an ownership structure different from that found in macroeconomic textbooks.

The first best solution to the problem of perverse behaviour of 'nobody's' banks and 'nobody's' industrial enterprises is, of course, privatisation, especially of banks. As this solution needs more time than was originally expected (apart from mistakes in privatisation strategy and tactics made by the government—see Beksiak & Winiecki, 1990; Gruszecki & Winiecki, 1991), some second best solutions are called for. This author has the following 'philosophy of intervention'. Reasonably well functioning markets do not require intervention (scarch for the Pareto optimum, unattainable in real-life conditions, does more harm than good). Where markets do not function reasonably well, intervention *vis-à-vis* a class of economic agents is preferable to that against specific economic agents (see also Williamson, 1985 and 1988). The worst thing that can happen to an economy is 'hands-on' management by policy makers that sooner or later dissolves into an 'everything-is-bargainable' type of economy. For Poland that would be a return to the dreaded past of the Soviet-type economy.

Therefore this writer suggested (Winiecki, 1991c) that commercial banks should be ordered to make a compulsory analysis of the cash flow of one class of economic agents, industrial SOEs, combined with an analysis of SOEs' mutual indebtedness. For it should be rememebered that one way for SOEs to survive has been not to pay their suppliers; and since suppliers had few other clients they have been reluctant to start bankruptcy proceedings. The analysis I propose would reveal which SOEs generate positive cash flow and—where they owe more than they are owed--

whether net cash flow would be enough to pay the bills in a reasonable timespan.

This is what commercial banks should have been doing all along but for reasons explained in the preceding sub-section they do not. Therefore, central bank guidance should force the banks to make such a simplified analysis of their clients' viability and, on the same basis, automatically refuse further lending to SOEs that generate negative cash flow or whose cash flow is lower than their (negative) balance of mutual indebtedness. (Some alternative measures could be applied instead, e.g. buying debt of that sort by the central bank, as suggested in a discussion by Alexander Jedraszczyk, or even abolition of all debt of SOEs *vis-à-vis* state banks and other SOEs (as suggested by Steinherr, 1991).

The emphasis on automaticity of bank behaviour has obvious reasons. It should help to avoid political pressure on commercial banks and resultant degradation of a proposed measure into yet another way of 'hands-on' management. There will certainly be some casualties of the automaticity but the lack of it would equally certainly be much costlier. There are, as stressed above, other unorthodox measures that could make orthodox monetary policy work better (at a minimum—in a non-perverse way). On these second best measures hinges the possibility of the success of monetary policy that at present seriously endangers the whole stabilisation programme.

'Autonomous' Macroeconomic Policy Errors

Apart from problems resulting from poor understanding of the interaction between state-owned banks and industrial enterprises, as well its consequences for macroeconomic balance, macroeconomic policy has suffered from 'autonomous' policy errors. I understand by the latter policy errors unrelated to micro-macro linkages analysed in the preceding section. The first and most striking (although not necessarily most fateful) have been interventionist 'itchings' at the macro level. The tendency to react to each and every change in macroeconomic indicators (in particular inflation) accentuated rather than smoothed the transition from near-hyperinflation *cum* stagnation to falling inflation *cum* recession to price stability *cum* recovery.

Nervous, overhasty decisions, particularly on monetary policy matters resulted first in accelerated recovery and later in stagnation and decline. The Polish economy went through a full cycle from recovery to recession in less than a year. Apart from adjustment costs in terms of the shift from old STE patterns of behaviour to market-type behaviour, enterprises had additionally to incur costs of adjustment to the changing cyclical situation of the economy. In the stylised pattern of the business cycle these adjustments pay back over the time-span of the (stylised) cycle. Within the framework of a cycle measured in terms of months rather than years only costs are incurred. Some part of the problems Polish SOEs are now encountering undoubtedly stems from extra costs incurred as a result of this 'compressed' cycle.

What is of analytical interest here is the extremely strong correlation between changes in monetary policy stance and output changes. Furthermore, the lag between the former and the latter is markedly shorter (and also seems less variable) than asserted by monetary theory. A look at Table 3.5, where interest rate changes are set against industrial output changes lagged by just one month, reveals a marked correlation between the two variables.

If this correlation is more than an ephemeral phenomenon, a whole range of questions should be raised. The first, of course, concerns the sources of such unusual sensitivity to changes in monetary policy. There is little theoretical and empirical groundwork in this respect (not surprisingly, given the short timespan of the transition), so that it is only informed guesses that can be offered here on the basis of knowledge of the traditional Soviet-type economy.

Enterprises in the STE, whether orthodox Stalinist or 'reformed' Hungarian or Polish-type, were extremely wasteful. Their inven-

Table 3.5

Interest Rate (Lagged One Month) and Industrial Output Rate
April 1990–June 1991

Month	Basic monthly lending rate of the central bank (lagged one month)	Industrial output monthly rate (preceding month = 100)
April 1990	10.0	98.5
May 1990	8.0	100.3
June 1990	5.5	104.9
July 1990	4.0	87.8
August 1990	2.8	107.6
September 1990	2.8	108.0
October 1990	2.8	100.4
November 1990	3.6	100.0
December 1990	4.6	103.2
January 1991	4.6	82.4
February 1991	4.6	100.8
March 1991	6.0	100.1
April 1991	6.0	91.7
May 1991	6.0	98.3
June 1991	4.8	

[a] Beginning with March 1990 rate.

Sources: as Table 4

tories were generally very much higher than those of their privately owned counterparts in the West. They used much more materials per unit of output (and per dollar of GDP). But they were always much more strictly controlled with respect to possession and use of monetary balances. This was the case quite apart from the inadvisability of keeping any large part of their current assets in the form of cash or demand deposits in a shortage-plagued economy.

This author's hypothesis is that at the beginning of the transition process SOEs in Poland found themselves short of money under the changed supply/demand conditions and resultant requests for prompt payment for deliveries. In the mature Western market economy a sudden increase in the firm's demand for cash would be met either by the sale of less liquid assets (various money market instruments such as treasury bonds, large certificates of deposit, etc.) or by short-term credit. Since enterprises in an STE did not have (and were not allowed to have) the former, they had to depend on the latter. However, the latter became extremely costly with the beginning of the transition programme—and macroeconomic restraint. True, they found some other sources of financing for the time being (see the first section) but overall, so to say, the 'level of monetisation' of Polish enterprises remained rather low relative to their Western counterparts. There are certain standard measures in analysing financial structure at the enterprise and/or industry level (see, e.g., Rybczynski, 1982, analysing structural change in British industry) but they cannot be used in direct comparisons owing to the existence of various distorting factors and incomplete data on SOEs' financial situation. Thus, the foregoing cannot be easily empirically proven. Nonetheless, I think that part of the problems of industrial SOEs stems from their unusually high sensitivity to interest rate changes.

The second 'autonomous' policy error of the government concerns the timing of the second round of restrictive macroeconomic policy. Apart from nervous reactions to monthly changes in the inflation rate, the decision to tighten monetary policy drastically through sharp rises in interest rates in October and November 1990 had momentous consequences. In actual fact it is this decision that pushed the Polish economy into the second recession in autumn 1990.

In the preceding section I criticised the rationale for this decision. What I see as a major 'autonomous' policy error is the timing of this decision. Let us assume for the sake of argument that the government was right in seeing the September 1990 increase in inflation *vis-à-vis* August 1990 as a sign of rekindled inflation and not as a return to the underlying inflation rate registered since March 1990. Was it then right, under the circumstances, to raise the central bank's basic lending rate from 34% to 54% on an annual basis just at that time, i.e. in October and November?

My answer is an unequivocal no. The government, conscious just like everybody else of the changes in Poland's trading relations with the Soviet Union and other ex-COMECON countries, knew at that time that the change from transferable ruble to convertible currency trade would dramatically reduce Eastbound exports; many talked then about a probable halving of exports in this direction.

Now, exports in 1989 amounted to 16.5% of GDP (measured according to SNA) and exports to COMECON countries to 5.8% of GDP. In 1990 exports increased while GDP fell, according to preliminary estimates, by 12%. Thus, the share of exports, including that of Eastbound exports, increased as well. Therefore it could easily be estimated that a halving of Eastbound exports in 1991 would create a strong recessionary impulse amounting to about 4-5% of GDP. With severe recession looming over the economy and expected to exert its influence in January 1991 the sharp rise in interest rates in late 1990 amounted to overkill. The economy came to a halt in October (possibly for seasonal reasons) and, more ominously, remained flat throughout the rest of the year under the impact of tightened monetary policy.

When the recessionary impulse from falling foreign demand came in January the economy fell over the precipice: industrial output declined by 18.3% in one month. Yet another increase in the central bank's basic lending rate in late January 'ensured' that the recession would continue. I regard the apparent inability of the macroeconomic team to correlate determinants of the macroeconomic situation at the turn of 1990 and 1991 as the biggest—and at the same time most easily avoidable—macroeconomic policy error.

In the same category of 'autonomous' policy errors I put excessive devotion to a fixed exchange rate in a highly inflationary economy. I myself accepted at certain point the argument advanced by Jeffrey Sachs that under near-hyperinflationary conditions stability of the exchange rate has a positive psychological impact on economic agents (a reflection of this argument could be found in Beksiak, Gruszecki, Jedraszczyk & Winiecki, 1989). But there is a world of difference between maintaining a fixed exchange rate for a few months at the start of the stabilisation programme and keeping a fixed exchange rate for the whole year in the face of a more than threefold rise in the CPI (and almost threefold rise in the quasi-WPI). Unfortunately, devotion to a fixed exchange rate is shared by influential international institutions, such as the IMF, that support a fixed exchange rate as part of the adjustment package. But again, knowledge of local conditions is valuable as it helps to avoid pitfalls that undermine the impact of the package.

A fixed exchange rate in the case of a temporarily disequilibrated Western market economy may put pressure on domestic producers not to raise prices because of the threat of cheaper imports. A fixed exchange rate is indeed anti-inflationary. However, this works reasonably well in the short run and with inflation rates in the range of, say, 5% to 15% on an annual basis. In Poland since March 1990 inflation rates on a monthly basis varied on average between 3% and 5%, with large monthly fluctuations. Under such circumstances maintaining a fixed exchange rate from January 1990 till May 1991 (in the face of quadrupling prices) undermined instead of improving the competitiveness of Polish enterprises. It is certainly necessary to inject competition into what had been a highly concentrated economy, but at the same time few enterprises, whether SOEs or privately owned, can succeed in reducing their costs by more than 60% within a year (this was the percentage by which the dollar's value fell in zloty terms).

A good saying the present writer once read is worth repeating here: 'Not every kick in the pants galvanises: some merely hurt'. An overdose of the medicine has threatened the bulk of industrial enterprises with bankruptcy. Once again ignorance of differences in local conditions in applying standard policy measures resulted in perverse effects. The injury is all the greater since, as this author stressed in the preceding section, it is better, not worse, SOEs that have been more adversely affected by monetary policy.

An obvious conclusion is that the fixed exchange rate regime should have been changed to a flexible exchange rate regime months ago or, at the very least, given the dominant Keynesian philosophy of the government's macroeconomic team, that the fixed exchange rate should have been smoothly adjusted in the face of the rapidly changing domestic price level. This theoretically sound rationale is, however, overwhelmed by very difficult technical problem of such adjustment. To answer the question when and by how much the exchange rate should have been changed is extremely difficult in view of the distorted prices before 1990.

Nonetheless, some benchmarks could be established. The government devalued the zloty substantially on 1 January 1990, in the expectation of rapid price increases after liberalisation of domestic prices. The devaluation in real terms was about 30% larger than the nominal one (as suggested by an even greater difference in a 'guesstimated' purchasing power parity for traded goods). That gave the government room for maintaining a fixed exchange rate for some time. Erosion of competitiveness became very strong at a certain point, though.

I think that a reasonable benchmark for managing the exchange rate could be established by reference to changes in domestic prices relative to black market (and later grey market) exchange rates in the past and the official rate in 1990 and 1991. These changes were notably uncorrelated, because the foreign exchange market rationally adjusted its expectations of future inflation and acted upon it by devaluing the zloty more quickly than either the government with respect to centrally set prices or SOEs with respect to decentralised prices. As the reference timeframe I suggest 1988, the last year before the transition that witnessed an export surge. Substantial devaluation in late 1987 resulted in a large increase in convertible currency exports in 1988 (by 17.4% in current US$). Regardless of the choice of benchmark, some benchmark should have existed for smooth adjustment of the exchange rate.

Delayed exchange rate adjustment also helps to explain the missing benefits of the second phase of the opening up of the Polish economy. International trade textbooks stress two-phased benefits. First, as selling abroad becomes more (or at all!) profitable firms shift a larger part of their output abroad. The second, and more important, phase comes when greater profitability entices existing firms in the export sector to invest to increase export capacity and new firms to shift resources to the export sector. However, shift of resources is rarely based on firms' own resources only and the second credit squeeze in autumn 1990 strongly discouraged investment. On top of that, the profitability of exporting was declining fast with the exchange rate unchanged and domestic inflation increasing by 3-5% on a monthly basis. Facing the double discouragements, the export shift petered out toward the end of 1990 and did not register any marked recovery in spite of a further dramatic fall in domestic demand and increased pressure to export.

Lastly, it is impossible to complete an overview of macroeconomic policy in the period under consideration without mentioning another stone around its neck that is wage controls. The present writer has criticised this particularly harmful measure in the context of the Polish transition programme so many times (see, *inter alia*, Beksiak, Gruszecki, Jedraszczyk & Winiecki, 1989; Beksiak & Winiecki, 1990; Winiecki, 1990a and 1990b), that he feels absolved fron taking up the subject thoroughly once again. Therefore only some aspects of the problem will be mentioned here. First of all, and this *ceterum censeo* should be repeated every time, wage controls shift the wage conflict from micro (enterprise) to macro (government) level, leading to unnecessary politicisation of wage claims. The harm done in the longer run heavily outweighs the benefits of such a policy in the short run (if there are any, as maintained, e.g., by Bruno, 1990; and Dornbusch & Simonsen, 1987; and others).

In the particular time and place of the Polish transition between mid-1990 and mid-1991 the government, instead of abandoning wage controls, chose the worst possible way, that of manipulating the rules established earlier by itself. Worse still, under strike pressures it did not abandon wage controls but reduced their impact by case-by-case concessions. Since concessions were usually given not to the most efficient but to the numerically and politically strongest, these concessions brought no efficiency gains (the opposite in fact was the case). Furthermore, the credibility of wage controls was seriously undermined, inviting more and more strike pressure.

Credibility of Economic Policy: The Missing Factor in the Government's Considerations

Since the late 1970s one of the hottest topics in economic theory has been the credibility of government economic policy. Concern with credibility stemmed from the fact that apparently reasonable policies did not bring about expected effects (or even resulted in perverse ones) when the government's policies were regarded by economic agents as not credible. Some theorists emphasised the time inconsistency of policies and their perception as being inconsistent by economic agents (see Kydland & Prescott, 1977), others analysed conditions that led economic agents to believe that policy makers had abandoned an interventionist stance in favour of a stable rule (see Barro & Gordon, 1983; and, in a slightly different context, Neumann, 1990); still others explained the persistence of intervention by underlining benefits to policy makers stemming from intentional ambiguity of their pronouncements and the feasibility of such ambiguity in the face of informational assymetry with respect to policy makers' intentions between policy makers and the public (see Cukierman, 1986; Cukierman & Meltzer, 1986; and Meltzer, Cukierman & Richard, 1990). The foregoing did not exhaust all strands of thinking about the credibility issue (see, e.g., contractarians' works with respect to uncertainty reduction through rules on policy making).

Whatever the achievements of various strands of economic theory, none of these was unfortunately taken into account in economic policy making by the Polish government in the transition period. Analysing its macroeconomic policies, one gets the impression that policy makers mistook political support for the government for credibility of particular policies. Regarding political support for the government as high, they apparently did not think it worthwhile to tailor particular policies with credibility in mind. As a result, no positive reinforcement for particular policies was gained from policy design.

Unfortunately, general support for a government of a given political colouring does not mean that behaviour of economic agents with respect to a particular policy will be in accordance with policy makers' expectations if the policy does not look credible. Monetary policy in 1990 serves as a good example here. The transition programme started announcing a restrictive macroeconomic policy stance. On the surface, words were followed by deeds: the interest rate was raised very sharply on 31 December 1989 to 36% for the month of January 1990. But in reality the signals were at best mixed.

As I emphasised in the second section, the government announced the need for a restrictive macroeconomic policy months in advance but at the same time did very little to stop the inflow of cheap money and real resources to SOEs before the 'big bang'. Real interest rates remained strongly negative from September till December 1989; cheap imports continued to flow in, fueled by an undervalued exchange rate till the last days of 1989. Judging by the most recent past, enterprises might have been partly justified in their expectation that the restrictiveness would be a temporary phenomenon and things would be 'back to normal' (in fact: abnormal) soon. Even after the beginning of the transition programme the government that abolished export earnings retention quotas did not in any way neutralise the money that SOEs later converted

Table 3.6

Term Structure of Interest Rates on Deposits in the Central Bank (Annual Rates)

Type of deposits	Until 30 January 1991	From 1 February 1991
Demand deposits	9	12
Time deposits:		
6 months	30	64
12 months	39	68
24 months	44	70

Source: Narodowy Bank Polski: *Sprawozdanie z Realizacji Polityki Pienieznej w I Kwartale 1991* (quartcrly), mimeo.

into zlotys and used as a cash balance support in the early months of 1990. Thus, signals continued to be mixed and supported the natural unwillingness to adjust. A wait and see, or minimum adjustment attitude on the side of most SOEs was not completely unjustified.

Mixed signals that undermined the credibility of macroeconomic restraint could have ended in the second half of 1990 as sources of financial support for enterprises (cheap inputs from the past, foreign exchange earnings converted into zlotys) began drying up. The credibility of the government's commitment to restrictive macroeconomic policy might have increased as a result. However, the government shifted to a more accommodative policy at about the same time (summer 1990). In consequence, SOEs got a strong signal that things might, after all, be moving 'back to normal': this obviously was not in fact true but such were the credibility-related consequences of policy change at this particular moment. And, let it be noted, the confusion resulting from the differences between government words and government deeds in summer and autumn 1990 (see the first section) did not add to the credibility of macroeconomic policy either.

In some cases policy makers themselves directly contributed to undermining the credibility of their own policies. Again, monetary policy is illustrative here. A look at the term structure of interest rates (see Table 3.6) reveals that the policy makers themselves did not believe in the success of their attempts to eradicate inflation. Time deposits in commercial banks for varying periods from one month to two years carry interest rates indicating strong expectations of accelerating inflation in the coming years.

Table 3.6 points to the fact that not only did commercial banks expect inflation to be higher the longer the timespan (because time deposits carried higher interest rates for three months than for one month, for six months than for three months, etc., with the highest interest rate for two years), but the spread was increasing throughout the October 1990-April 1991 period. This term structure did not come from nowhere. It was dictated primarily by the interest rate paid to commercial banks for their deposits with the central bank. In this manner the central bank undermined the credibility of its own policy.

This is not the end of credibility-undermining actions by policy makers. Exchange rate policy is not free from such problems either. The increasing divergence between stability of the exchange rate and rapid inflation caused a lot of speculation about imminent devaluation of the zloty. Firm denials to the contrary, reality had to reassert itself at a certain point. But immediately after devaluing the zloty in May 1991 by 16% policy makers again began their earlier declarations about defending the new parity of the zloty. Obviously, their pronouncements carried much lesser weight thereafter, all the more so as the zloty was still perceived to be overvalued.

Overall mixed signals and resultant low credibility of macroeconomic policy in themselves constituted a factor reinforcing weak adjustment, quite apart from other sources contributing to this weakness. Macroeconomic policy was not, however, the only area where credibility did not positively reinforce government policy (to say the least).

Trade with the Soviet Union was another example, although more one of omission than commission. As exports to the USSR (and other ex-COMECON countries) collapsed after the shift to convertible currency trade, various ideas for temporary support were floated in government circles. To the best of my knowledge, however, none of the proposed schemes had any built-in credibility-reinforcing mechanism. The whole idea of temporary support is based on the premise that SOEs dependent on the Soviet market should have the time necessary for adjustment to new, more demanding conditions of convertible currency trade. Therefore, whatever the scheme, it should have a declining degree of support built into it from the start.

Assuming, for example, support through tax relief for SOEs which exported, say, more than 30% of their output Eastward, tax relief extended over some 18 months should give the full percentage of planned relief for the first six months, two-thirds of the relief for the next six months and only one-third for the last six months of the scheme. In this manner, even if the first six months were wasted without any adjustment whatsoever, the reduction of tax relief would serve as a signal that the government was serious about adjustment. The credibility of this particular policy would be enhanced and, consequently, prospects for adjustment would improve.

Credibility may be equated with a stock that, like any other, may increase or decrease as a result of policies pursued. Increase or decrease take place at a rate that is somehow related to the distance between policy pronouncements and actual policy actions. The smaller the distance, the more the stock increases and *vice versa*. In the case of governments of long standing or political groupings returning to power with a certain record of past policy making, there may be quite a substantial stock of credibility and one or two slip-ups will not draw down the stock too heavily. But this is not true of a new government, no matter how strongly supported on a general political plane. Regardless of strong general support, a few credibility-reducing mistakes may draw a given policy's credibility down sharply, as the stock of credibility from which to draw is not large. Moreover, whatever credibility has been there, it was given on (easily recallable) credit. Polish government policies have been strongly—and adversely—affected by lack of understanding of this problem.

In Place of Conclusions

I began with a reference to an earlier assessment concerning the first half of 1990 (Winiecki, 1990a). Prospects for success were at that time rather high although I cautioned against easy optimism and criticised the privatisation cum demonopolisation part of the programme (see Winiecki, 1990a; and Beksiak & Winiecki, 1990). The year between mid-1990 and mid-1991 changed the prospects markedly. Accumulating policy errors, as well as perverse results of some policies, undermined prospects for success in the short run.

Inflation did not subside, while the economy slid into a second recession in so many years. Worse still, the structure of output got progressively worse as better enterprises faced bankruptcy much more often than politically strong but economically less efficient ones. Supported by advice based on ignorance of the STE, the government's macroeconomic team kept to an unchanged course that may result in the threat of bankruptcy for a large proportion of SOEs.

Now, if it is dozens of SOEs that simultaneously go bankrupt, the government may weather the storm somehow. The situation changes dramatically if numbers increase from dozens to hundreds (or more). Faced by looming collapse of a large part of industry, the government may give in to the pressure for relief. However, under the weight of large numbers relief cannot be anything else than wholesale. As every enterprise gets relief because large numbers overwhelm the government's and everybody else's ability to differentiate between classes of more and less deserving SOEs (see the second section of the paper), the effort and sacrifice already made may largely be lost. The stabilization programme

102

would have to start again and with much less credibility (as well as with much lower willingness to continue belt-tightening).

Yet the prospect of failure and the need for a second round of stabilisation medicine may not necessarily be the end of the dismal story. Not only the government but also the idea of a rapid transition to the market system may become discredited in the process. Some populist, 'third way' type of coalition that would radically change the direction of transition might then come to power. If this were to happen, prospects for success would disappear in the medium run as well. Years might have to pass before another, this time hopefully more sensibly executed programme aiming at the same target, a capitalist market economy, became a political reality.

References

Barro, R.J. & Gordon, D.S. (1988), 'A positive theory of monetary policy in a natural rate model', *Journal of Political Economy*, 91, pp. 589-610.

Beksiak, J., Gruszecki, T., Jedraszczyk, A. & Winiecki, J. (1990), *Zarys programu stabilizacyjnego i zmian systemowych*. See English version (1990): 'Outline of a Programme for Stabilisation and Systemic Change', in: *Polish Transformation: Programme and Progress*, Centre for Research into Communist Economies, London.

Beksiak, J. & Winiecki, J. (1990), 'A Comparative Analysis of Our Programme and the Polish Government Programme', in: *The Polish Transformation: Programme and Progress*, Centre for Research into Communist Economies, London.

Bernholz, P. (1990), 'Necessary and Sufficient Conditions to End Hyperinflations', Institut für Volkswirtschafs, Universität Basel, mimeo.

Bruno, M. (1990), 'High inflation and nominal anchors', Bank of Israel, Jerusalem.

Cukierman, A. (1986), 'Central bank behavior and credibility—some recent theoretical developments', *Federal Reserve Bank of St Louis Review*, 68, May, pp. 5-17.

Cukierman, A. & Meltzer, A.H. (1986), 'A theory of ambiguity, credibility and inflation under discretion and assymetric information', *Econometrica*, 54, September, pp. 1099-1128.

Demsetz, H. (1980), *Economic, Political and Legal Dimensions of Competition*, North-Holland, Amsterdam.

Dornbusch, R., Sturzenegger, F. & Wolf, H. (1990), 'Extreme inflation: dynamics and stabilization', *Brookings Papers on Economic Activity*, No. 2, pp. 1-84.

Dornbusch, R. & Simonsen, M.H. (1987), 'Inflation stabilization with incomes policy support: A review of the experience in Argentina, Brazil and Israel', Group of Thirty, New York.

Furubotn, E.G. & Pejovich, S. (1972), 'Property rights and economic theory: survey of recent literature', *Journal of Economic Literature*, 10, December.

Gomulka, S. (1991), 'Tworcza destrukcja' (Creative destruction), *Zycie Gospodarcze*, No. 18.

Gruszecki, T. & Winiecki, J. (1991), 'Privatisation in East-Central Europe: a comparative perspective', *Aussenwirtschaft*, 46, 1.

Narodowy Bank Polski (1991), 'Informacja o liczbie przedsiebiorstw, ktore wedlug oceny bankow nie posiadaja zdolnosci kredytowej' (Information on Enterprises, which according to Banks Lost their Creditworthiness), Warsaw, mimeo.

Jensen, M.C. & Meckling, W.H. (1976), 'Theory of the firm: managerial behavior, agency cost and ownership structure', *Journal of Financial Economics*, 3, 4.

Kydland, F.E. & Prescott, E.C. (1977), 'Rules rather than discretion: the inconsistency of optimal plans', *Journal of Polifical Economy*, 85, June, pp. 473-492.

Meltzer, A.H., Cukierman, A. & Richard, S.F. (1990), *Political Economy*, New York.

Neumann, M.J.M. (1990), 'Precommitment to stability by central bank independence', Prepared for the Fourth Hayek Symposium on Knowledge, Evolution and Competition, Freiburg, 9-12 June, mimeo.

Rybczynski, T.M. (1982), 'Structural changes in the financing of British industry and their implications', *Nat-West Quarterly Review*, March.

Steinherr, A. & Peree, E. (1991), 'Privatisation in Eastern Europe: some concrete proposals', Paper prepared for Kieler Woche Conference on Transformation of Socialist Economies, Kiel, 26-28 June, mimeo.

Williamson, O.E. (1985), *The Economic Institutions of Capitalism*, Free Press, New York.

Williamson, O.E. (1988), 'The logic of economic organization', *Journal of Law, Economics and Organization*, 4, Spring, pp. 65-93.

Winiecki, J. (1989), 'Large industrial enterprises in Soviet-type economies: the ruling stratum's main rent-seeking area', *Communist Economies*, 1, 4, pp. 363-383.

Winiecki, J. (1990a), 'Post-Soviet-type economies in transition: what have we learned from the Polish transition programme in its first year', *Weltwirtschaftliches Archiv*, 126, 4, pp. 765-790.

Winiecki, J. (1990b), 'Walesa must resist the "reflation" siren song', *Wall Street Journal*, 21 December.

Winiecki, J. (1990c), 'Kilka uwag o gospodarce waznych dla nowej ekipy ekonomicznej rzadu' (A Few Remarks on the Economy Importance for the Economic Management Team of the New Government), Warsaw, December, mimeo.

Winiecki, J. (1991a), *Resistance to Change in the Soviet Economic System, Property Rights Approach*, Routledge, London.

Winiecki, J. (1991b), 'Political Economy of Privatization, *Kieler Arbeitspapiere*, Institute für Weltwirtschaft, Kiel.

Winiecki, J. (1991c), 'Inflacja i wzrost gospodarczy a polityka rzadu' (Inflation, Economic Growth and Government Policy), Warsaw, March, mimeo.

Winiecki, J. (1991d), 'The inevitability of a fall in output in the early stages of transition to the market', *Soviet Studies*, 43, 4, pp. 669-676.

4 Expected and unexpected developments in stabilization and liberalization

Introduction

Literature on the transition of former Soviet-type economies (post-STEs for short) is growing fast, although, given the pace of developments, it is still mostly at the articles and mimeo papers stage, with few serious books on the subject. Debates are already beginning to shape up: 'shock therapy' versus gradualist approach, the sequencing of transition measures, choice of privatisation methods, etc. They promise to fill pages of economics journals for years to come. The shift from centrally managed (and allegedly centrally planned) economy to the market system has become a veritable 'new frontier' for the profession.

What the present writer regards as missing in this avalanche of articles and papers on the subject is an attempt at stock-taking. After all, the Polish transition programme was formulated in autumn 1989 and more than two years have passed since it began to be implemented. The same by and large applies to Hungary. After extensive preparations the Czecho-Slovak programme started in January 1991. Yugoslavia, Bulgaria and Romania, albeit with some reservations (mostly due to their unfinished political transition to the post-communist era, see Winiecki, 1991a), also contributed something to the growing pool of evidence.

There exists, then, an accumulation of evidence against which various concerns of theorists, including those dominant in implemented stabilization cum liberalization programmes, can be assessed. This paper is an attempt at such an early assessment. The present writer looked at theorists' concerns from two different angles: first, whether certain developments expected by theorists did or did not happen and, second, whether certain developments that did happen were expected by theorists. This approach is summarised in tabular form in Table 4.1.

The selection of issues that are seen as being of concern to theorists is of necessity personal. Another theorist would, in all probability, make a somewhat different selection (especially in the —of necessity—more arbitrary choice of developments that surprised theorists). But even with all possible arbitrariness the approach yielded interesting insights.

One of the most important is that only a small part of theorists' expectations as to the problems of transition did, in fact, materialise in a manner expected by a theory. Transition to the market turned out to be a much more uncharted journey than had been imagined by believers in simple (one is tempted to say simplistic) recommendations transplanted from economies with different institutional characteristics.

What was Expected to Happen and Actually Happened

As signalled already, the list of developments in the transition process that had been expected to happen and did happen is rather short. Moreover, even when certain developments did take place they were more often than not qualified by various 'buts'.

Expectations based on the standard stabilization programme recommended nowadays by the IMF (the new orthodoxy called the 'heterodox programme') suggest that hyperinflation is reduced sharply once restrictive monetary policy is put in place and an attempt is made substantially to reduce the budget deficit and particularly its financing through resort to the printing press. In fact, Jeffrey Sachs, arguing on the basis of Bolivian experience (1987), tended to be even more optimistic and expected inflation to disappear almost completely (although this was not the case in Bolivia itself, see, e.g., Bernholz, 1988).

This more extreme version did not materialise but Yugoslav and Polish hyperinflation did in fact end. But inflation, although reduced substantially, got stuck at levels higher than in known successful cases of stabilisation policies (Chile, Bolivia, Israel, Mexico). High monthly inflation rates (e.g. in Poland, apart from outliers, 3-4% per month from April 1990) strongly affect macroeconomic policy, which in turn affects the performance of a post-STE in transition.

Considerations underpinning the same standard stabilization programme generate associated expectations of reduction in budget deficit. This reduction, let alone elimination, takes place at a markedly slower rate. But the pattern in post-STEs has been the reverse of that registered earlier elsewhere. In country after country initial balancing of the budget after the start to transition was achieved almost overnight with surprising ease. However, after some time, usually in the second year of the transition programme, surplus turned into deficit—and usually a fast growing one. This happened in Poland and Hungary in the second year and a deficit is looming in Czecho-Slovakia in 1992. Quite obviously, some factors not taken into account in the underlying theory of stabilisation have intervened forcibly in the fiscal area. These issues will be considered at length in Section IV.

The same reverse pattern has been observed also in the case of export expansion as an effect of external liberalization. This has been assumed to take place once (1) exchange controls are lifted; (2) substantial devaluation of the (heavily overvalued) national currency is instituted and (3) distorting non-tariff barriers to trade are eliminated. These measures are expected to reveal true comparative advantages. However, the process of finding export markets under newly revealed comparative advantages takes more time than ordering goods from abroad that were unavailable before liberalization owing to—now eliminated—exchange controls. Therefore, import surge is generally expected to precede export surge (see, e.g., Krueger, 1980, and her later writings).

This is the logic behind the stabilisation funds set up under the aegis of the IMF. These funds were to help post-STEs in the early transition period to withstand the pressure on foreign exchange reserves caused by increased imports, since exports were supposed to pick up much more slowly. The need for stabilization funds has been stressed from the very beginning of post-STE transition and, surprisingly, as late as 1991 (see, e.g., Asselain, 1991; and Portes, 1991).

The present writer regards this concern as surprising, for by 1991 it should have been clear that export surge materialises rather early: a steep growth in exports is registered almost immediately after liberalization. In the only case where it did not, Czecho-Slovakia, the fall in imports exceeded that in exports. Thus, in the latter case too there was no need to draw on the stabilization facility.

What threatens export transition is not, as widely expected, an early import surge with its attendant political pressures to reimpose exchange controls and distortionary non-tariff barriers but a *late* import surge, following the export surge. The threat comes from the inconsistency of fixed (or 'pegged') exchange rate, regarded as an indispensable nominal 'anchor' in the standard stabilization programme, with steady export expansion based on comparative advantages. This is what, i.a., was observed by Edwards (1992) in the Chilean case.

As the fixed exchange rate is used as an anti-inflationary weapon the policy bias favours maintaining it for too long. In the extreme case of Poland it was maintaned for 17 months during which prices rose by 300%. It is quite clear that such a great difference between inflation rates in Poland and in Poland's main trade partners could not be made up by efficiency-increasing, cost-reducing measures. An increasing overvaluation of the zloty ensued, with the resultant loss of competitiveness.

The effect on the trade pattern was dramatic. In the first half of 1990 exports amounted to 119.7% of those in the first half of 1989 while imports were only 54.1%. In 1990 as a whole exports rose to 140.9% of those in 1989 while imports were equal to 106.3% In the first nine months of 1991, however, exports were 117.9%, while imports rose to a whopping 196.5% of the level in the equivalent period of 1990.

In Hungary the situation was exactly the same, although overvaluation grew more slowly, there (owing to lower inflation differentials *vis-à-vis* the country's main trading partners). Nonetheless, imports were 112%, the corresponding figures for the first half of 1991 *vis-à-vis* that of 1990 were 127% and 177%. In Yugoslavia import pressures were so strong toward the end of 1990 that the currency had to be sharply devalued and its convertibility suspended.

The issue involved is not well presented in textbooks on international economics but the benefits of opening up the economy come in two phases. Phase one is rather short and associated with liberalization of foreign exchange and foreign trade. Domestic producers realise that shifting some of the output to foreign markets will bring higher profits. The result is an increase in exports from the *existing* capacities and a resultant one-off increase in the value added. This is what happened in post-STEs immediately after external liberalization.

But this is only the beginning of the benefits in question. As comparative advantages are revealed some goods become permanently more profitable than others. Over time there is, as a consequence, a *shift* of production factors from less to more profitable activities. A more profitable export-oriented sector becomes increasingly bigger and contributes more value added. However, if this is to become a permanent feature of the newly opened economy the real exchange rate should remain reasonably stable.

And this is what post-STEs that chose a fixed exchange rate regime have missed. The second phase of reaping the benefits in question did not materialise. The real exchange rate fluctuated strongly as overvaluation superseded the undervaluation existing at the start of the transition and production factors did not shift to more profitable uses (for the very simple reason that these uses were rapidly losing their profitability). Partial corrections made on an *ad hoc* basis did not help very much and in themselves undermined the credibility of the desired structural change in favour of the export-oriented sector.

The preceding considerations give a foretaste of the stock-taking attempted in this paper. As can easily be seen, even those not so numerous developments that duly happened as expected did not follow the pattern observed under earlier stabilisations. The following two sections on expected developments that did not happen and unexpected developments that took most of the profession by surprise reinforce this assessment.

Expected Developments that Did Not Happen

One more general comment should be made before the beginning of the overview on unexpected developments, be it those that were expected to happen but did not or those that took most of the profession by surprise. In neither case were surprises always due to the uniqueness of post-STE transition. The underpinnings of alternative interpretations allowing us to 'expect the unexpected' were already in place in some writings or could have been deduced from the existing literature. Consequently, their adverse effects on economies in question might have been to some extent avoided or alleviated, had that knowledge been applied in transition processes.

In fact the same may be said about the unexpected developments that duly happened—but not according to the established pattern of the past. There has been an extensive critique of the orthodoxy of a fixed or pegged exchange rate as a solution in the short run coming form economists of varying theoretical persuasions (see, i.a., McKinnon & Mathieson, 1981, repeated in McKinnon, 1991; Murrell, 1992, with respect to all 'nominal anchors'; Walters, 1991; and Winiecki, 1991c). In fact one of the founders of the new stabilisation orthodoxy also began criticizng of late the use of exchange rates as a means of controlling inflation (Dornbusch, 1990). And consequences of an exchange rate 'anchor' for export performance of a liberalizing economy could easily be deduced from textbooks of international economics.

One of the issues that greatly concerned theorists (and those at the helm of transition programmes) was monetary overhang, forced savings in the hands of the population—a legacy of decades of repressed inflation under the STE regime. Solutions proposed ranged from outright confiscation (so-called 'monetary reform'), consolidation as debt, conversion into financial or real assets or correction through the process of price liberalization.

But in fact only the first and the last were seriously considered by theorists, while in all countries considered here (Poland, Yugoslavia, Hungary and Czecho-Slovakia) correction through price liberalisation was chosen—wisely—by the respective decision makers. For although there exists a theoretical equivalence between these two options, outright confiscation is politically untenable in newly evolving democracies, as well as requiring knowledge that does not exist about the size of monetary overhand (see Edwards, 1992).

In any case monetary overhand turned out to be a non-issue after the start of transition. This assessment applies not only to countries where preceding hyperinflation had already wiped out a large part—if not all—of monetary overhang, i.e. Poland and Yugoslavia, but also to the remaining countries in transition. Actually, in the former countries an *opposite* problem emerged. Since the overhang was wiped out, the restrictiveness of monetary policy did not need to be as strong as it was (Beksiak & Winiecki, 1990). As households tried to rebuild savings to the desired levels even at the cost of further reducing their already reduced consumption, decision makers were free to pursue a somewhat less restrictive macroeconomic policy than that aimed *inter alia* at eliminating the already nonexistent monetary overhang.

The Damocles' sword of forced savings, however, overshadowed actual developments, with a resultant larger nominal decrease in consumption than was desirable for general turnaround in the supply/demand relationship under new rules of the economic game (on the rationale for macroeconomic restraint at the start of the transition going beyond the elimination of disequilibrium and, more specifically, forced savings, see i.a. Winiecki, 1990a).

Another widely feared development that did not materialise was widespread bankruptcies. Although over time more and more SOEs, as well as Soviet style pseudo-cooperatives, were regarded as decreasingly creditworthy, bankruptcies were almost nonexistent. When they happened at all they usually affected small firms.

The foregoing should not be construed to mean that the performance of non-privately-owned firms was better than expected. The oppose in fact was the case (see the next section). But various factors of an economic and political nature slowed down the adjustment process under the market rules.

Two factors were decisive for the almost complete absence of selection through bankruptcy. The first is in my opinion related to another nominal 'anchor' of the standard stabilisation programme, i.e. wage controls. In all the programmes in question wage controls became a norm, and wage controls slow down badly the needed adjustment process (Beksiak & Winiecki, 1990; and Walters, 1991). Thus, quite apart form the theoretical inconsistency of using more than one nominal variable as an 'anchor' (see Claassen, 1991), nominal wage rate controls have had other adverse consequences.

On the one hand, by restraining efficient as well as inefficient SOEs from increasing employment and wages, they petrified the existing output structure. On the other hand, by restraining inefficient SOEs from increasing wages they reduced considerably the probability of bankruptcies. Although this has been precisely one of the reasons for their introduction, the 'nanny' role of wage controls undermined the credibility of macroeconomic restraint and the new rules of the (market) game.

The second factor is associated with the extended tradition of 'soft' budget constraint of SOEs (see Kornai, 1980; 1986) that did not completely disappear after the transition. In all countries under consideration, with some exceptions concerning Hungary, large SOEs continued to hold strong political clout thanks to their sheer size and resultant unemployment consequences. The political economy of 'soft' budget constraint under the transition regime will be discussed, however, in the next section of this paper.

Yet another major threat to stabilisation that did not materialise is an import surge, that was supposed immediately to follow external liberalisation. As stressed earlier, this was generally the rationale behind the establishment of stabilization funds in economies liberalisating their foreign economic relations. But import surges preceding export expansion did not happen and the explanation for this could be found in the comparative economic systems literature (see Winiecki, 1983; 1985; repeated in Winiecki, 1988, and Ellman, 1989).

STEs were characterised by very strong import pressures because SOEs preferred imports from Western market economies to lower quality domestic products (or those from other COMECON countries). Since they paid the same price for products of differing quality they always pressed for imports originating from the West. Also, they tried to ensure excessive inventories of imported high quality inputs. It was part of the system-specific high inventory-to-output ratio policy of state enterprises that could afford to disregard the usual financial constraints.

With the new rules of the game, price differentiation introduced an element of choice between domestic and imported goods. If the price differential was larger than the quality differential SOEs chose domestic over imported inputs. Also, they started reducing high levels of inventories that became more difficult to finance under the new rules, reinforced by macroeconomic restraint. A not unexpected result, in the light of the preceding considerations, was a sharp fall in imports, exceeding the aggregate fall in domestic output in all countries in question (Czecho-Slovakia being an exception). Stabilization funds were left unused everywhere.

Unexpected Developments that Surprised Decision Makers and the Economics Profession

There are serious problems with expectations based on the standard stabilization programme. In the model underlying the 'heterodox' programme (see Dornbusch & Fischer, 1986) policies aiming at elimination of hyperinflation (and severe disequilibria) concentrate on reduction of aggregate demand through restrictive monetary policy and rapid decrease in budget deficits. Severe restraint, i.e. the 'shock treatment', is preferred as more credible than gradual restraint. This credibility is reinforced by nominal 'anchors' that, by freezing some nominal variables, help to drive down inflationary expectations.

A natural, one way say textbook consequence should be a fall in output. The model says nothing either about the degree of macroeconomic restraint necessary to eliminate hyperinflation or severe disequilibrium, nor about the resultant fall in output. This is what one might expect from the programme based on the new orthodoxy with the extent of output fall corresponding, intuitively, to the level of hyperinflation or disequilibrium. It is, then, even more surprising that empirical analysis of earlier applications of such programmes showed that they resulted in rather shallow recessions or, as in the case of Israel, even a small expansion (see, i.a., Bruno, 1986 and 1991; Kiguel & Liviatan, 1990; Corbo & Solimano, 1991).

Programmes, the applications of which seem to contradict the underlying theory shoud be immediately suspect (and certainly do not deserve the name of orthodoxy, whether old or new!). Be that as it may, almost nobody among the protagonists of the standard stabilization programmes expected the *extent* of output fall that took place in almost all countries in question plus Eastern Germany. Hungary, which decided in favour of gradualism, performed differently with respect to the initial output fall (although not with respect to the aggregate output fall over the period under consideration).

The initial fall in industrial output in the first year of the transition amount to over 40% in Eastern Germany and some 25-30% in Poland and Czecho-Slovakia. Only in Yugoslavia was it much lower (over 10% in 1990), as macroeconomic policy became traditionally lax later in the year, when effects of the squeeze began to be felt.

It has been posited by this author on several occasions (Winiecki, 1990a, 1991b and 1991d) that a substantial fall in output was to be expected on the basis of the existing knowledge on the behaviour of enterprises in the STE. The very change from a wasteful Soviet economic system entails an *autonomous* fall in output, quite apart from the degree of restraint of macroeconomic policy or external environment.

The 'mystery of vanishing output' is in fact rather simple. The STE was known for its persistent shortages, to which economic agents, especially SOEs enjoying 'soft' budget constraint, adapted by hoarding inputs, fixed assets and labour. The best known are probably very high inventory-to-output ratios. To give an example, according to Shmelev & Popov (1989), the ratio in the USSR in 1985 stood at 82%, while in the United States it was 31% in the same year.

Quite obviously, once the beginning of the transition brings about the reversal of the traditional supply/demand relationship, SOEs begin to adjust to the new conditions of excess supply by drawing down their inventories and simultaneously lowering or cancelling new orders for both inputs and machinery and equipment. Thence stems the fall in domestic demand for and, consequently, output of raw materials, intermediate products, lathes, instruments, construction and transport equipment, etc.

Not only state enterprises but also households, with their harder budget constraint, adjust to the new relationship. In fact they adjust much faster for that very reason. The re-emergence of goods in the shops is met by purchases of smaller quanities of, e.g., food products. Earlier people bought larger quantities whenever they got hold of them, no knowing when they would be able to buy the next batch. Part of these larger quantities was later spoiled.

The foregoing leads to the conclusion that transition from the STE to the market system is bound to entail a *larger* output fall than in other cases of stabilisation *cum* liberalization. Of course, not *all* output fall could be ascribed to the departure from the wasteful Soviet economic system. Therefore it is a legitimate question to ask whether the size of output fall that these countries registered was necessary to achieve the initial aim of the stabilization programme, i.e. sharp disinflation, or was excessive. And the question is valid regardless of whether those who pose it understand or accept the implications of the foregoing considerations or not.

The concept of a credit crunch in the state enterprise sector was advanced (Calvo & Coricelli, 1990) to explain why enterprises reduced output owing to the lack of resources to purchase necessary inputs. The explanation implies that output in Poland (although it could apply elsewhere as well) was driven below the level of demand. However, Castberg (1991), for example, points out that the concept of credit crunch cannot explain the state of generalized excess supply dominant on the Polish market.

The present writer takes an intermediate position between those who maintain, with Calvo & Coricelli, that reflation would accelerate recovery and those who say, with the prevailing orthodoxy, that although severe recession was engineered on the demand side (macroeconomic restraint), it must be overcome by supply side measures (structural adjustment).

The Calvo & Coricelli explanation applies perhaps to a limited extent and only in industries that were caught awkwardly in a period of seasonally high credit demand at the start of the transition. Facing initially extremely high interest rates they reduced output below demand level (with the differential filled by imports). This dilemma is typified by the food industry.

Furthermore, a markedly larger output fall in consumer goods producing industries indicated that other forces were at work besides the inventory drawdown. For it is SOEs rather than households that needed to adjust more under the shift from excess demand to excess supply regime (given their larger inventories thanks to their 'soft' budget constraint). Therefore it is rather a nominal 'anchor', that is wage controls, that might have affected the level of wages, demand for and, consequently, output of consumer goods producing industries. Thus, some room for relaxation of restictive macroeconomic politics, including wage controls, did exist there.

This is not intended to be a critique of decision makers but rather support for the thesis that the very limited knowledge of the structure and behaviour of the economy in transition from the centrally-managed STE to a market-type one leaves a lot of room for possible mistakes. Under such circumstances the use of nominal 'anchors' is of limited value, to say the least (on this point see Murrell, 1992).

One of the most important developments—and strongly adverse—developments has been the impact of an unhealthy nexus of state-owned banks and state-owned industrial enterprises on the performance of economies in transition (Winiecki, 1991c). 'Nobody's' banks, that did not care much for the creditworthiness of their clients or the riskiness of projects submitted, tended to lend on an inertial basis to those to whom they lent in the past, that is first of all to the largest SOEs. They were also sensitive to political pressures to support 'important' enterprises. On the other hand, 'nobody's' enterprises borrowed almost regardless of the level of interest rates. This applied to to a much greater extent to the largest SOEs, which were more accustomed than other firms to being bailed out of trouble by communist regimes.

These problems highlighted the neglected role of the financial system, that would also entail the search for a solution to the bad debt incurred by SOEs under the old regime. Without cleansing the balance sheets of the banks from bad loans made under central planning, simultaneously with the similar procedure with respect to industrial enterprises, restructuring and privatization turned out to be well nigh impossible. In actual fact, even the expected impact of macroeonomic policy would become doubtful. Few analysts seemed to have been aware, however, of the necessity of early and rapid reform of the financial system (for exceptions, see Brainard, 1990; Marer, 1990; Rybczynski, 1991).

In fact, it transpired over time that monetary policy applied within the framework of the standard stabilization programme in countries with a strikingly different property rights' structure generates outcomes that are at odds with textbook-based expectations. Not only adverse outcomes of monetary policy came as a surprise; the spillover effects that affected strongly—and again adversely—the state budget similarly surprised both practitioners and theorists.

As explained briefly in Winiecki (1992), a not unreasonable assumption of monetary policy under the standard stabilization programme is that each post-STE enters the transition in a state of greater or smaller disequilibrium and therefore restrictive monetary policy is required. An even better reason in post-STEs is to send a signal to economic agents that the era of persistent excess demand has come to an end. A shift to an excess supply regime is generated through the monetary squeeze.

What is conspicuously missing in this reasoning is the typically neoclassical neglect of the consequences of monetary squeeze in economies where the property rights structure is drastically different from that in the textbooks. For there is a world of difference between situations where SOEs generate 10% or even 30-40% of GDP and those where they produce anything from 90% to 100% of the product (as in the case of Czecho-Slovakia at the start of transition, for example).

The consequences were very similar everywhere. Owing to the unhealthy nexus between 'nobody's' banks and 'nobody's' industrial enterprises which we have already stressed, extended monetary squeeze has so far brought largely perverse results. Not only, as stressed already, did output fall somewhat more than necessary but also its structure deteriorated. Contrary to textbook expectations that monetary squeeze eliminates the least efficient firms, under the overwhelmingly dominant state ownership the reverse has been true.

Banks continued to lend first of all to their traditional clients, that is, the largers SOEs, with the consequence that smaller, usually more efficient, ones were crowded out of the credit market. The political clout of the largest state enterprises additionally ensured that they remained least affected by the squeeze. As the largest but historically least efficient firms continued to have the easiest access to credit from equally dominant state-owned commercial banks, their output losses were relatively lower. And since it has been the smaller and better SOEs that faced the toughest credit squeeze, the output of the latter often fell by a larger percentage. Output structure thus progressively worsened. This is best explained in Winiecki (1991c) and Walters (1991).

The worsening output structure under prolonged monetary restraint generated yet another surprise, namely fiscal crisis in the second year of the transition. This has come about in the most dramatic way in Poland but the budget deficit increased in Hungary in 1991 too and this author's assessment is that it may materialise in Czecho-Slovakia as well.

I have already stressed that the pattern of fiscal developments has so far been the opposite to the one found in earlier cases of stabilisation. The budget was balanced relatively easily at the very start of stabilisation in each case, while over time the situation progressively deteriorated.

This surprising result is again rooted in the legacy of the past. SOEs historically maintained large inputs inventories. Accelerating inflation and growing disequilibria in the last years of the STE regimes accentuated this tendency (see Shmelev & Popov, 1989, for the USSR; and Winiecki, 1990a, for Poland).

Now, the new rules of the game freed prices at which products were sold, while inputs for these products had been bought earlier at much lower, controlled prices. Therefore, although output fell and capacity utilization was low, profitability remained high. As budget revenue depended to a very large degree under the inherited tax structure on state enterprises' profits, the stream of revenue was sufficient to cover expenditure. This is what happened in Poland, Yugoslavia and Hungary in 1990 and in Czecho-Slovakia in 1991.

But prolonged monetary squeeze, with its perverse effects on the enterprise sector, undermined SOEs' profitability. On the one hand, profits of better, more efficient SOEs fell sharply. On the other, wasteful giants, living on subsidies and never-to-be-repaid credits, rarely contributed much to state coffers. In fact, the opening up of these economies generated some competitive pressures and resulted in further worsening of these giants' financial performance. Thus, their contributions declined, too.

As revenue declined budget deficits began to increase. The relatively least affected has been Hungary, which began reforming its tax system earlier, in the late 1980s. It entered the transition with a more diversified tax system that included also personal income tax and VAT. Therefore the fall in SOEs' profitability that also occurred in that country did not affect aggregate budget revenue so strongly.

All countries so far tried to avoid re-igniting inflation by printing money. Therefore they adjusted their budgets downward to keep deficits within manageable limits. An unintended but nonetheless surprising consequence of these developments has been a fast decline of budget-to-GDP ratios in all countries concerned (again, except Hungary, where the decline has been much less pronounced for reasons already explained).

There are, however, limits to the decline of budget-funded activities. The resistance increases and shifts the issue from the economic to the political arena, undermining the whole transition process (since in the industrial sector also there is a lot of bitterness, not least because better rather than worse SOEs have their backs to the wall).

Alongside the emerging urgency of reform of the financial system, reform of the tax system proved to be another urgent priority. Both came largely as a surprise, since neither stabilisation nor liberalisation were seen as strongly dependent on financial or tax reform, at least in the shorter run (on tax reform see, however, Kaminski, 1989, and McKinnon, 1990 and 1991).

Unexpected and Unnoticed Developments

The set of unexpected developments considered in the preceding section has been more extensive than that of expected developments, whether those that did happen or those that did not. Unexpected developments are, however, even more numerous. For one should take into account the fact that the preceding section listed only those surprising developments that have already received growing recognition.

On the other hand some developments that the present writer did not consider in the previous section have, in his opinion, taken place, even though the economics profession seems to continue arguing about them as if nothing happened. In other words, certain developments were not only unexpected but also passed so far

Table 4.1

Expected and Unexpected Developments that Happened or Did Not Happen in Post-STEs' Transition

	Expected	Unexpected
Happened		a
Did Not Happen		X

[a] There is a need for further subdivision of this class of developments:
those that were noticed by the profession and those that passed largely unnoticed.

unnoticed. In terms of Table 4.1 they also belong to the upper right hand quadrant: the class of unexpected developments that happened (whether this was noticed or not).

At least two debates continue with much fervour, although developments in post-STEs seem by now to have decided their outcome. The first debate centres on the question whether the return to the capitalist market economy is the only game in town. Market socialism, an alternative long cherished by the left, has been one of the choices debated, while preference for labour-managed firms—a variation on the theme—has had not only intellectual but also practical support within some post-STEs and outside.

This overview of expected and unexpected developments in the post-STE transition to the market is not a proper place to discuss the merits and demerits of alternatives to capitalism (the present writer did that elsewhere, see Winiecki, 1990b and 1991e). What is worth noting here is the fact that the gist of the debate in question seems already to have been decided on the basis of post-STEs' 1990-1991 experience.

Contrary to the pronouncements of decision makers in some post-STEs on shifting back to the capitalist market economy, what we have seen so far in these countries has been by and large market socialism: a world of state-owned enterprises (banks, etc.) affected by the manipulation of market-type policy instruments: interest rates, taxes, exchange rates and the like. Furthermore, most of the unexpected and strongly adverse developments, as well as the absence of some expected beneficial developments in countries in transition, have been due precisely to the fact that state-owned economic agents behave differently form privately owned ones (see, i.a., Walters, 1991, and Winiecki, 1991c). A version of market socialism with labour-managed firms was also tried in 1990 in Yugoslavia (and to some extent in Poland in 1990-1991) and registered similar failure.

Thus, the failures of the transition are largely due to the market-socialist nature of these economies. It is only with the advance of privatization, both through transformation of the state sector and the expansion of private firms, that this market-socialism nature will gradually disappear and, at a certain stage, a capitalist market system will become a reality. Discussing alternatives to capitalism as if these alternatives had not been tried already (and failed!) gives the debate a slightly surrealistic tinge.

The present writer is of the opinion that an even more frequently pursued debate on gradual vs. rapid transition to the market has already been decided by the 1990-1991 developments. What has been called a 'shock therapy', 'big bang', etc.—and criticised by gradualists—has been a critical mass of stabilizing, liberalizing and other institution-building measures necessary to obtain a degree of coherence among the rules of the game, ensuring at least a tolerable level of performance in the transition period.

It transpired, however, since late 1989 that what was thought to be a critical mass in fact fell short of expectations in this respect. Most of the problems these economies encountered stemmed not from the fact that they did too much at one moment, i.e., at the starting point of the transition, but *too little*. Even on the basis of this paper's assessment once could add the need to initiate immediate changes in the financial system (cleansing the balance sheets of state banks and state enterprises) and at least short term modification in the inherited tax system (reducing budget dependence on state sector profits).

As stressed by this author elsewhere (Winiecki, 1991f), demand for capitalist market economy institutions is very great from the start, while supply—in spite of strenuous efforts—necessarily lags behind. Improved performance is a result of reducing the gap between demand for and supply of these institutions. Graphically it is shown as a decrease of the distance between the S1 and D lines in Figure 4.1.

Spreading the range of necessary measures over a longer period, as suggested by 'gradualists', has important implications for performance. It means even less coherence among the rules of the game than that offered by the critical mass approach, for the gap between demand for and supply of institutions will be initially larger and the time needed to reduce it substantially longer as well (as shown by the lines D and S2 in Figure 4.1). It also means that the improved performance will come later.

To close this section it is worth noting that part of the gradual versus rapid transition debate seems to be generated by muddled thinking about the problem at hand. Some discussants tend to confuse two different types of decisions taken at the start of the transition programmes in post-STEs. The first type is a decision about a range of liberalizing and other institution-building measures that are to be taken at the start. The second is about a degree of macroeconomic restraint: level of interest rate, extent to which subsidies are to be reduced to narrow budgetary deficit, or extent of

Figure 4.1

Demand and Supply of Market Economy Institutions

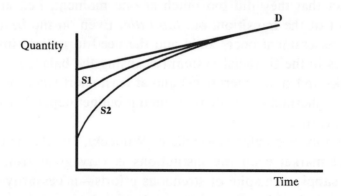

exchange rate devaluation. Some discussants criticise mostly the second type of measures.

However, their critique of that type does not make them 'gradualists'. In this author's view, recent experience of post-STEs in transition has already decided the debate in question in favour of a concentrated broad range of stabilizing, liberalizing and other institution-building measures taken in the shortest possible time span and against a gradual approach.

On the other hand, decisions on the degree of macroeconomic restraint at the start of the transition are related to the degree of disequilibrium and strength of inflationary pressures present in these economies. One may, of course, discuss the appropriateness of one degree of restraint or another or of the length of the time span of restraint but this, by itself, has little to do with the preference for gradual transition.

In Place of Conclusions

The stock-taking of expected and unexpected developments analysed against the background of theorists' concerns, however imperfect and selective, yields nonetheless an unambiguous picture with respect to the basics of the transition process. A very large, in fact dominant, part of the developments assessed came as a surprise of one type or another to the economics profession. Either some developments expected to take place did not or, more often, unexpected developments affected—strongly and usually adversely—the post-STE transition.

The stock-taking, let it be noted, has been selective not only through this author's judgement of what constitutes important developments but also owing to the omission of some aspects of the transition. One such, overwhelmingly important, aspect has been privatisation. It was consciously omitted from consideration here because it is a very large issue area that deserves a stock-taking of its own (this is, incidentally, attempted in Winiecki, forthcoming).

In itself the dominance of surprises over developments expected on the basis of the received theory should not be seen as something extraordinary. The transition from collectivist cum totalitarian regime, with its special economics-politics interface (see Winiecki, 1987, 1991), has been an uncharted path, where no standardised, textbook-based solutions would be expected to apply without thoughtful adaptation.

The fact that they were applied—in the completely different institutional environment of post-STEs—in the form of standardised ('heterodox') IMF stabilisation programmes created certain expectations that simply could not be fulfilled. In consequence these programmes became as much part of the problems of transition as of the solution.

References

Asselain, J. (1991), 'Convertibility and Economic Transformation', *European Economy*, No. 2 (Special Edition), pp. 215-241.

Beksiak, J. & Winiecki, J. (1990), 'A Comparative Analysis of Our Programme and the Polish Government Programme', in *The Polish Transformation: Programme and Progress*, Centre for Research into Communist Economies, London.

Bernholz, P. (1988), 'Hyperinflation and Currency Reform in Bolivia: Studied from a general perspective', *Journal of Institutional and Theoretical Economics*, Vol. 144, pp. 747-771.

Brainard, L. (1990), 'Strategies for Economic Transformation in Eastern Europe: The role of financial reform', Conference on 'The Transition to a Market Economy in Central and Eastern Europe', OECD, Paris, 28-30 November, mimeo.

Bruno, M. (1986), 'Curing Hyperinflation', *Economic Policy*, April, pp. 379-402.

Bruno, M. (1991), 'From Sharp Stabilization to Growth: On the political economy of Israel's transition'. A paper prepared for the European Economic Association conference on 'Economists as Policy-Makers', Cambridge, 1 September, mimeo.

Calvo, G.A. & Coricelli, F. (1990), 'Stagflationary Effects of Stabilization Programs in Reforming Socialist Countries: Supply side vs. demand side factors', IMF, Washington, Septermber, mimeo.

Claasen, E.M. (1991), 'Sequencing and Timing of Stabilization Policies in the East', International Economic Conference on Building the New Europe', Rome, 7-9 January, 1991, mimeo.

Castberg, C. (1991), 'The Polish Stabilization, 1989-1991: Why the recession was created on the demand side, but must be solved on the supply side', Aarhus University, Institute of Economics, mimeo.

Corbo, V. & Solimano, A. (1991), 'Chile's Experience with Stabilization Revisited', IBRD Working Paper WPS 579, mimeo.

Dornbusch, R. & Fisher, S. (1986), 'Stopping Hyperinflations: Past and Present', *Weltwirtschaftliches Archiv*, Vol. 122, pp. 1-47.

Edwards, S. (1992), 'Stabilization and Liberalization Policies in Eastern Europe: Lessons from Latin America', in Clague, Ch. & Rausser, G., eds., *The Emergence of Market Economies in Eastern Europe*, Basil Blackwell, Oxford.

Ellman, M. (1989), *Socialist Planning*, Cambridge University Press, Cambridge.

Kaminski, B. (1989), 'Reforming the Tax System in Poland: General prescriptions of tax design'. Paper prepared for the Brussels' Burean of 'Solidarity', College Park, Md., mimeo.

Kiguel, M. & Liviatan, N. (1990), 'The Business Cycle Associated with Exchange Rate-Based Stabilization', IBRD Working paper PRE 513, mimeo.

Kornai, J. (1980), *Economics of Shortage*, North-Holland, Amsterdam.

Kornai, J. (1986), 'Soft Budget Constraint', *Kyklos*, Vol. 39, No. 1.

Krueger, A.O. (1980), 'Trade Policy as Input to Development', *American Economic Review*, Vol. 70, May, No. 2, pp. 288-292.

Marer, P. (1990), 'Pitfalls in Transferring Market Economy Experience to the European Economies in Transition', Conference on 'The Transition to a Market Economy in Central and Eastern Europe', OECD, PAris, 28-30 November, mimeo.

McKinnon, R.I. (1991), *The Order of Economic Stabilization, Financial Control in the Transition to a Market Economy*, The Johns Hopkins University Press, Baltimore.

McKinnon, R.I. & Mathieson, D. (1981), *How to Manage a Repressed Economy*, Princeton Essays in International Finance No. 145.

Murrell, P. (1992), 'Evolution in Economics and in the Economic Reform of the Centrally Planned Economies', in Ch. Clague & G. Rausser, eds., *The Emergence of Market Economies in Eastern Europe*, Basil Blackwell, Oxford.

Portes, R. (1991), 'The Transition to Convertibility for Eastern Europe and the USSR', Centre for Economic Policy Research, Discussion Paper Series, No. 500, January, mimeo.

Rybczynski, T.M. (1991), 'The Sequencing of Reform', *Oxford Review of Economic Policy*, Vol. 7, No. 4, pp. 1-9.

Sachs, J. (1987), 'The Bolivian Hyperinflation and Stabilization', *American Economic Review*, Vol. 77, May, No. 2, pp. 279-283.

Shmelev, N. & Popov, G. (1989), *The Turning Point: Revitalizing the Soviet Economy*, Doubleday, New York.

Walters, A. (1991), 'Monetary and Fiscal policy and Aid in the Transition', a paper prepared for the Mont Pelerin Society meeting in Prague, 3-6 November, mimeo.

Winiecki, J. (1983), 'Central Planning and Export Orientation', *Oeconomica Polona*, Nos. 3-4.

Winiecki, J. (1985), 'Central Planning and Export Orientation in Manufactures (Theoretical considerations on the impact of system-specific features on specialisation)', *Economic Notes* No. 2.

Winiecki, J. (1987), 'Why Economic Reforms Fail in the Soviet System, A Property rights-based approach', Seminar Paper No. 374, Institute for International Economic Studies, Stockholm, mimeo.

Winiecki, J. (1990a), 'Post-Soviet-Type Economies in Transition: What have we learned from the Polish transition programme in its first year?', *Weltwirtschaftliches Archiv*, Vol. 126, No. 4, pp. 765-790.

Winiecki, J. (1990b), 'No Capitalism Minus Capitalists', *Financial Times*, 20 June.

Winiecki, J. (1991a), *Resistance to Change in the Soviet Economic System*, Routledge, London.

Winiecki, J. (1991b), 'Costs of the Transition that Are not Costs: On the non-welfare reducing output fall', *Rivista di Politica Economica*, Vol. 81, No. 6, June, pp. 85-94.

Winiecki, J. (1991c), 'The Polish Transition Programme at Mid-1991: Stabilisation under Threat', *Kieler Diskussionsbeiträge*, 174, Institüte für Weltwirtschaft, September.

Winiecki, J. (1991d), 'The Inevitability of a Fall in Output in the Early Stages of Transition to the Market: Theoretical Underpinnings', *Soviet Studies*, Vol. 43, No. 4, pp. 669-676.

Winiecki, J. (1991e), 'Theoretical Underpinnings of the Privatisation of State-Owned Enterprises in Post-Soviet Type Economies', *Communist Economies and Economic Transformation*, Vol 3, No. 4, pp. 397-416.

Winiecki, J. (1992), 'Eastern Europe: An Ominous Pattern', *Wall Street Journal*.

Winiecki, J. (forthcoming), *Polish Privatisation in Comparative Perspective*, J. C. B. Mohr (Paul Siebeck), Tübingen.

Part Two

Privatizing and Shaping Institutional Infrastructure

5 Privatization theory: Basic underpinnings

The experience of state-owned enterprises (SOEs) in Soviet-type economies (STEs), as well as that of state-owned enterprises in less developed countries and in the West contributed greatly to better appreciation of private ownership as a factor crucial for efficient, wealth-creating growth of output. It is worth noting that the careful qualifier 'efficient, wealth-creating' applied to output growth is the direct consequence of the performance of STEs. Before the emergence of these economies growth was regarded as wealth-creating by assumption. At the same time the experience of SOEs also brought about growing appreciation of the role of private ownership in fostering innovation, another source of increased well-being achieved through the enlargement of the social opportunity set.

For both reasons, strongly reinforced by the overall decline and recent collapse of Soviet-type economies, *historical* arguments about the superiority of markets *cum* private ownership are nowadays established well enough. Therefore, in what follows I present only *theoretical* arguments in favour of private enterprise, and *eo ipso* in favour of privatization.

Although in my opinion theoretical arguments are no weaker than historical ones, they are largely of a more recent vintage and, as such, somewhat less firmly established within academe and the political elite. Furthermore, as various arguments were put forward by different strands of economic theory, theoretical underpinnings of privatisation are not always well integrated into a coherent whole. This article is an attempt at integrating various strands of theory from this particular vantage point. Moreover, since the focus is on the comparative analysis of various forms of enterprise ownership within the market system, as a rationale for privatisation, it is the enterprise rather than the economic systems level of analysis that is dominant in my considerations.

Furthermore, a comparative approach as applied here requires precise formulation of what is being compared and within what framework. I follow the comparative institutions approach of Demsetz (1969). Relevant choice is made between alternative real institutional arrangements, rather than between ideal institutions and existing, and therefore imperfect, institutions. Using Demsetz' terminology, I try to avoid a 'Nirvana' approach.

The framework within which real institutional arrangements (private enterprise, SOE, labour-managed firm, etc.) are compared concerns their relative wealth-creating capability. The definition used here includes wealth creation both by improved resource allocation and by enlargement of the social opportunity set. The framework of comparison includes also the impact of the state on the performance of enterprises characterised by different forms of ownership.

Early Arguments in the 'Calculation Debate'

The first clearly formulated arguments in favour of private enterprise as a basic unit of the efficient economy were formulated long ago in the famous (albeit widely misperceived) calculation debate. (What follows is largely based on Lavoie, 1985a.) Ludwig von Mises as early as 1923 criticised 'as-if' owners representing departments within the central planning organisation who, according to Heimann's (1922) scheme, traded with each other as if they were owners of the means of production. According to Mises, they could conceivably buy and sell as if they were owners, but this behaviour would not be able to replicate the behaviour of real owners (Mises, [1923] 1936, pp. 518-520).

The price formation process is based on the rivalry of private entrepreneurs. In his comments on the 'artificial markets' Mises argued later in 1936 that 'it is not possible to divorce the market and its functions in regard to the formation of prices from the working of the society based on private property of the means of production'. He stressed the role of incentives:

> The motive force of the whole process which gives rise to market prices for the factors of production is the ceaseless search on the part of capitalists and entrepreneurs to maximise their profits... Without these private owners the market loses the mainspring that sets it in motion and keeps it in operation. (1936, pp. 137-138)

Being able to attend to 'daily business routine' is the limit of what 'artificial markets' with as-if planners can offer. The roles of entrepreneur, investor and speculator are inseparable from private ownership. Mises allowed that the routine may be efficiently reproduced by planner-managers (which turned out to be an excessively optimistic thesis—see the next section). However, 'one cannot play speculation and investment', he maintained (1949, p. 709). The speculators and investors 'expose their own wealth, their own destiny ...'. Planners are not constrained that way while bidding for resources.

The foregoing establishes Mises as a predecessor of the modern property rights theory in this respect. In accordance with the latter, public officials neither bear the entire cost nor can appropriate the full benefits resulting from their actions. 'The penalty-reward system associated with public ownership provides public decision makers with weaker incentives to pursue efficient outcomes' (Pejovich, 1990, p. 33).

Parallel to Mises, Robbins (1934) and Hayek (1935) offered a similar approach to the relative efficiency of alternative forms of ownership. The former used almost the same terminology of socialist managers 'playing at competition' and the necessity of continuously moving beyond routine tasks. However, non-routine tasks require property rights assigned to a multitude of entrepreneurs, which was clearly incompatible with 'ownership and control at the centre' (1934, p. 154).

Hayek also regarded the system where socialist managers do not pay for their mistakes as a 'pure illusion' ([1935], 1948, p. 176). And to the argument already quoted, about missing incentives to behave in an efficient manner, he added also an early argument about dispersed knowledge. Although the required knowledge does exist it cannot be used efficiently by a central planning organisation in the absence of the competitive process. For it is through this process and resultant market prices that the dispersed knowledge is revealed (Hayek, 1945). Thus, the early formulations of the growth-of-knowledge philosophy of science (see the last section of this article) were applied to economics in conjunction with the stress on private, i.e. dispersed ownership as a condition for using the dispersed knowledge efficiently.

These early views, stressing fundamental weaknesses of alternative economic systems (central planning and market socialism), as well as those of public ownership, were largely neglected by both antagonists in the 'calculation debate' and policy makers. The former never addressed the question of incentive structure differences between public and private ownership. Not only were the implications of dispersed, non-communicable knowledge of the multitude of market participants for central planning not addressed but what was really at issue remained widely misunderstood.

Many theorists were convinced that the 'calculation debate' proved Mises wrong on the issue of a theoretical model of a socialist price system (for a selected list see Lavoie, 1985a), while others regarded the existence of central planning in the USSR as a historical argument against Mises' central thesis. Elliot (1973, p.

211), for example, concluded that 'private ownership is not now regarded as a logically necessary system ... for economic calculation'. A question could—and should!—be raised as to what is economic calculation, as opposed to, say, accountant's or engineer's calculation. This question, however, has never been discussed by either side of the debate.

Practitioners were even more impressed by the alleged successes of Soviet planning (the fictitious nature of numbers produced by Soviet and other communist regimes was not yet questioned at the time), as well as by wartime intervention in the economy in the West. Public ownership in the goods-producing sector became regarded not only as legitimate in economic terms but was seen by enthusiasts as being better able to follow government-formulated rules of financial performance. Some made the even more controversial claim that SOEs outperformed private enterprises (few of them reversed their earlier judgement, see however Pryke, 1971 and 1981).

Property rights became a marginal issue in economic debates of the first quarter of a century after World War II. As an illustration of the thesis, an influential book by Shonfield (1965) devoted a few pages only to the ownership issue but half of the book to varieties of planning in the West. Many others at that time were writing about an era of collectivism. Over time, however, various strands of economic theory supplied ever more arguments with which to build upon the foundations laid by Mises, Hayek, Robbins and others. Changing economic realities and, somewhat more slowly, perceptions of these realities now made their reception easier both in academe and in the polity.

Comparative Enterprise and Resource Allocation

This section is concerned with comparative wealth-creation capability through resource allocation. However, given the peculiarity of the enterprise's position in the STE, the resource allocation issue is augmented by considerations with respect to actual use of resources once they were allocated and resultant differences in wealth-creating output growth of the same publicly owned enterprises under alternative economic systems. None the less, the bulk of the argument pertains to alternative enterprise arrangements within the framework of the market system.

These arguments come mostly from property rights theory and associated strands of neo-institutional economics (in the sense of Eggertsson, 1990). The best starting point seems to be the Jensen & Meckling (1979) argument that the neoclassical production function should be augmented by the structure of property (and contracting) rights in order to explain differential performance of enterprises endowed with the same quantity (and quality) of production factors, material inputs and technology. As they stress rightly, 'it is of little importance to know that it is physically possible to produce 100 units of a good with some given level of factor inputs if no one in the system has the incentive to do so' (p. 471). Different incentives under alternative property rights arrangements give rise to various problems affecting the performance of enterprises. In analysing them I largely follow Jensen's & Meckling's (1979) approach.

Crucial in this respect is the *control* problem, i.e. owner(s) control over the performance of the firm. It is here that the superiority of privately owned firms over any other alternative form of ownership is most clearly visible. In proprietary firms managed by their individual owners, in partnerships and in limited liability (closed) companies problems arising out of separation of ownership from control are avoided. Owner(s)-manager(s) bear the full wealth effects of decisions they take (however, as the number of partners or shareholders in a closed firm increases, a common property problem begins to emerge; see below).

The joint-stock company (open company or corporation in American terminology) with its widely dispersed private ownership is affected by the control problem owing to the separation of ownership and management. The emphasis on high costs to share-

holders of monitoring managers of joint-stock companies domi-
nated the scene since the influential book by Berle & Means
(1932). However, more recent theoretical developments reversed
the judgement by stressing the role of competitive markets that
constrain managers from pursuing objectives other than that of increasing the wealth of the shareholders. The cost of constraining
pursuit of these other objectives, variously defined in the neo-institutional literature as shirking (Alchian & Demsetz, 1972), the
agency problem (Jensen & Meckling, 1976) and opportunistic behaviour (Williamson, 1975, 1985), is reduced by an active stock
market.

> Insofar as share prices reflect the present value of the ex-
> pected future consequences of current managerial policies,
> market evaluation protects shareholders from a situation in
> which management has less concern for their wealth.
> (Pejovich, 1990, p. 61)

If managerial decisions are seen as damaging to the profitability
of the firm, they may activate a sequence of moves such as increased sale of shares by dissatisfied shareholders, subsequent fall
in share price (as supply exceeds demand), takeover by a new
group of shareholders and management shake-up.

As can be easily seen, competitive markets tend to work in conjunction with each other. Without the market for takeovers (or,
alternatively, market for corporate control) stock market signals
could result only in lower bonuses resulting from lower profitability for managers pursuing their own objectives. If managers'
on-the-job consumption exceeds the difference between high
profitability and low profitability bonuses, then this constraint on
management will not be very effective in the short to medium run.
The takeover threat increases the efficacy of the constraint.

Finally, the competitive market for managers reinforces the constraint on managerial behaviour. Managers not only respond to
threats (such as the threat of takeover with its consequence for
their current position) but also to opportunities. Their prospects

for managing more profitable and/or larger firms offering higher compensation in the future depend crucially on their present performance. This performance is continually scrutinised by the stock market through share prices. This, in turn, induces managers not to veer too far from the legitimate goal of managerial activity.

Thus, the problem of control in privately owned joint stock companies is largely alleviated by competitive markets that—taken together—improve owners' position *vis-à-vis* managers by reducing managerial discretion. No such solution is available, however, in the case of SOEs. The SOE, or, more precisely, the publicly owned firm (state-owned, local government-owned, etc.) is different in its incentive structure from the privately owned firm. It is owned collectively by all citizens, or all inhabitants of a given community (municipality, county, etc.). Since it is owned collectively, citizens or inhabitants of a given community cannot sell their shares in a SOE to display their dissatisfaction with its performance. No signals comparable with those affecting privately owned joint-stock companies are received by collective owners. Also, given the non-existence of a market for takeovers of SOEs, such signals could not in any case be followed by takeover, weeding out of inefficient and/or opportunistic management, and, in consequence, improved performance.

Now, although citizens or inhabitants of a given community do not have individualised claims to the residual income, they are all affected by the performance of the firm (through lower or higher taxes dependent on that performance). Their only way to display dissatisfaction is to leave the country or the community, on the one hand, or to influence the situation through active participation in the political process. Either way, the costs of these actions are usually very high relative to obtainable benefits (after all, one individual bears only a small fraction of the total costs of bad performance). Given weak owners' control and high costs of doing so (high transaction costs), inefficiencies in the performance of publicly owned firms are expected to both be greater and last longer than in privately owned firms.

The problem of control is strongly present in the Yugoslav labour-managed firm as well. In these firms, let us recall, capital assets are society-owned (effectively, state-owned), while the employees have the right to use these assets and distribute residual income arising out of this use. Also, they have the right to hire and fire the management. In contrast to property rights analysis of SOEs, the same type of analysis with respect to labourmanaged firms has been very extensive (cf. de Alessi, 1982, in the case of the former and Furubotn & Pejovich, 1972 and 1974; Furubotn, 1976; Jensen & Meckling, 1979). Analysts stress varied control-related difficulties.

Firstly, the decision-making process is pursued by employees who are not specialised in running a firm. Their control over management is of necessity less efficient than that of the board of directors in a joint-stock company. Secondly, quite apart from low level of competence of employees (relative to specialised overseers), the decision-making process is burdened with much more uncertainty than in any type of privately owned firm. There are many divergent interests among employees based on their age, family size, etc. The outcome of their voting on various issues (investment, social overheads, etc.) is dependent on the conflict resolution capability of such an institutional arrangement, which is not easily satisfied by the one man one vote rule. Thirdly, the fact that employees hire and fire the management team affects the control issue in yet another manner. Managers have incentives to substitute policies beneficial to the employees for those maximising the value of the firm in order to improve their chances for reelection. The abstract owner, society, is unable to intervene effectively (various kinds of state intervention proved to be ineffective).

The common property problem affects the performance, albeit to a different degree, of various enterprise arrangements, be they privately or collectively owned. Only two forms of private ownership are completely free from adverse effects of non-exclusive property rights: private proprietary firms and joint-stock companies. As the number of partners in partnerships and owners in

141

limited liability companies increases, so does the common property problem because the benefits of combining ownership and management functions correspondingly decline (see Eggertsson, 1990).

Publicly owned firms are apparently free from the common property problem, since an abstract owner is represented by a well defined administrative unit (treasury, city council, etc.). This creates insurmountable problems analysed later but of a different kind from those of common ownership.

In contrast, labour-managed firms face common property disincentives to undertake some projects that increase the present value of the firm. It is employees, not the abstract owner (society) who decide about resource allocation. Whenever a project entails not only an increase in capital but also in labour, existing workers have to share the cash flow from past projects with newly hired workers. Therefore, from among projects that increase the present value of the firm only those may be undertaken that increase the cash flow per worker. As Jensen & Meckling (1979) point out, theoretically they may even undertake projects that decrease cash flow as long as there is a proportionately larger decrease in employment (the peculiar employment feature of the Yugoslav labour-managed firm was noted long ago in a different context, see Ward, 1958).

An employee share ownership plan (ESOP) firm of the closed company type, that is with shares that are non-transferable outside the firm or with a preemption right for the firm to purchase shares before employees offer them for sale on the open market, is a privately owned firm in terms of property rights theory. However, given a large number of owner-employees, its problems are often nearer to those of a labour-managed firm than a partnership or limited liability company (similar to ESOP in their respective legal forms).

The ESOP firm copes better than the labour-managed firm with the control problem, although given the number of owners involved not as well as a partnership or limited liability company.

However, it shares the common ownership problem with the labour-managed firm, even if the kind of projects that may not be undertaken is different. In the case of an ESOP firm it is projects that increase the present value of the firm by reducing (rather than increasing) employment that may be rejected owing to the resistance of threatened employee-shareholders. In theoretical terms they may be rejected if the income stream from future wages of threatened employees during the lifetime of the project is higher than the income stream from dividends of the same employees (a rather common situation) and if these employees constitute a sizeable part of the total employee-shareholders (a less common situation).

The *horizon* problem pertains to the conflict between owner(s) desired pattern of consumption and expected income stream from investment made in the firm. If owner(s) display a stronger preference for current consumption than is implied by the market rate of interest, then some projects that maximise the present market value of the firm will not be undertaken because of the unacceptably long time horizon of the income stream.

The horizon problem appears in private proprietorship and, to a lesser extent, in partnerships and limited liability companies, while joint-stock companies are free from that problem. Fama & Jensen (1985) emphasise that where firms are scrutinized by the stock market and shares receive market (unbiased) evaluation, owners can always rearrange their portfolios to suit their time preference of consumption (trade shares for other financial assets to correlate their income stream with the preferred pattern of consumption). This is not possible in proprietorships, partnerships and closed limited liability companies. Therefore, the joint-stock company arrangement efficiently minimises the conflict between utility maximization by its owners and maximization of the present market value of the firm.

Publicly owned firms are also free from the horizon problem but for different reasons. It is not minimisation of conflict owing to well-functioning financial markets but disregard of conflict that is at the root of the non-existence of the horizon problem in these firms. Large-scale, long-term projects are decided by bureaucrats running the overseeing administrative unit or by management with its approval. They may decide on the issue in complete disregard to the impact on the present value of the firm. Thus, the freedom from the horizon problem is achieved at a high efficiency cost.

Labour-managed firms suffer heavily from the horizon problem. Since the horizon that employees apply in their decisions is determined by their employment in the firm, there is a marked preference for projects with shorter-term pay-off periods. Many projects with longer pay-off periods will not be undertaken. Therefore, there is a built-in bias in favour of current consumption *vis-à-vis* investment in labour-managed firms. Moreover, as stressed i.a. by Jensen & Meckling (1979) and Pejovich (1990), employees have a strong incentive to seek long-term bank credits for all projects, even those with a shorter pay-off period, in order to shift the stream of income forward to increase current consumption, while simultaneously shifting the burden of repaying credit onto the next generation of workers.

An ESOP firm suffers to a smaller extent from the horizon problem. Owner-employees' horizon is longer than that of employees in a labour-managed firm owing to the opportunity to continue to own shares after termination of employment. Thus, investment projects with varying pay-off periods are not treated differently on that basis alone (as in labour-managed firms). However, to the extent that owner-employees display a time preference for consumption that is in conflict with the market rate of interest, their project selection affected in the same manner as that of proprietors, partners in partnerships and owners of limited liability companies.

The *risk diversification* problem concerns specialisation in risk bearing by individuals who usually display differing degrees of risk aversion. This affects owners of proprietary firms who invest a large share of their human and financial capital in their own firm, while portfolio theory suggests that individuals displaying relatively strong risk aversion should reduce risk by diversifying their asset ownership across firms and financial instruments to obtain an income stream that is not dependent on any one asset. Thus, the proprietor may avoid certain more risky investments that would increase the present market value of the firm.

This theoretical disadvantage, cited, for example, in Fama & Jensen (1985), is, however, more hypothetical than real. Owners of private proprietary firms are on the average more entrepreneurial, not less, and *eo ipso* more ready to take risk than anybody else. There is a natural selection process that on the whole makes owners of proprietary firms greater than average risk takers. As a result, high risk aversion among them is a psychological impossibility. It should also be rejected on empirical grounds, since the rate of return on fixed assets is on average not lower in owner-managed proprietorships.

As the number of private owners increases in partnerships and closed, limited liability companies, their investment in their firms decreases as a share of their total wealth. In consequence, the risk diversification problem decline in importance. Again, the open, joint-stock company displays a strong advantage over all other forms of private ownership in this respect. Shareholders may easily diversify their portfolios to suit their varied degrees of risk aversion.

The publicly owned company is in a complex situation in this respect. On the one hand, decision makers (bureaucrats or managers) need not diversify across firms and types of assets since they do not invest financially in the publicly owned firm. Their portfolio, if any, is independent of their performance as bureaucrats or managers. But on the other hand they may not undertake projects that are seen as too risky and, as such, endanger their prospects for continued employment. Risk bearing in such a firm is differentiated not by the degree of own capital involvement but by the relative cost of failure. The latter is very low in the case of command from above and high in the case of own initiative. Also, the larger the scale of the project, the greater the cost of failure for the manager. Therefore, it is easily predicted that the probability of undertaking a project increasing the present market value of the firm (that is, the hypothetical value in the case of a publicly owned firm) is *ceteris paribus* inversely proportional to the scale of the project.

There is, according to de Alessi (1982), yet another diversification argument pointing to the disadvantage of the firm under consideration here (he uses the term 'political firm' rather than publicly owned firm). In the case of private firms individuals can rearrange their portfolios, specializing in ownership of firms they know more about. This is impossible in the case of publicly owned firms. Citizens or inhabitants of a given locality cannot sell their rights to, say, one such firm and buy those to another, of which they have some specialized knowledge. As voters they are part-owners of all the publicly owned firms in their country and locality. Lack of specialization creates an additional inefficiency.

Employees in a labour-managed firm face serious constraints on diversifying their 'portfolio'. They cannot specialize according to the degree of risk bearing in ownership of assets appropriate for each of them in this respect. Furthermore, they are forced by the nature of their claims to bear an aggregated risk, since both their basic wage and share in distributed profits are dependent on employment in a given labour-managed firm.

The ESOP firm employees again fare somewhat better than those of the labour-managed firm. Thanks to their well assigned property rights, employee-shareholders are able to specialise to some extent by selling some (a part of) their shares in a given ESOP firm and buying other assets. However, their income from employment and from the remaining part of their shares (where share ownership is a requirement) are affected by the problem of unnecessarily aggregated risk.

Finally, the *entry* problem needs to be considered within the framework the relative efficiency of resource allocation under alternative enterprise arrangements. It is a standard assumption that the free entry of new firms is an important factor contributing to efficient production through competitive pressure. However, the inclusion of the entry problem requires a slight redefinition of the field of analysis. So far I have analyzed relative performance of alternative enterprise arrangements in a market economy where alternatives compete to survive.

To underline the important role of free entry, each basic type of ownership is analysed as an exclusive one within the market economy. In this manner competition exists in a market economy with privately owned firms only: proprietorships, partnerships, limited liability companies, ESOP firms, joint-stock companies, etc. Publicly owned companies and Yugoslav labour-managed firms are exclusive species in their respective market (or quasi-market) economies.

Thus, privately owned firms enter the market spontaneously on the basis of decision of their owner-managers, partners, owner-shareholders, etc. Their decisions are based on the expectation of positive profits higher than those obtained elsewhere. However, if free entry (free in the sense of the absence of state-imposed barriers) is a standard for the capitalist market economy, this is not the case in the other two market regimes.

In the market economy with publicly owned firms it is a non-market, that is, a political decision that gives rise to the establishment of a new firm. Since decision makers do not bear wealth consequences of their actions, the number of firms will be indeterminate: it may just as well be too large as too small. Efficiency conditions will not be satisfied.

In the Yugoslav labour-managed firm the entry problem is unequivocal. In the capitalist market economy entrepreneur(s) establishing a new firm can count on capturing all residual income from that firm. Incentives for prospective entrepreneurs remain strong. In the labour-managed economy any employee who wants to incur costs involved in establishing a new firm has to weigh them against the prospect of obtaining $1/N$ of the residual income (where N is the number of employees in a prospective firm). With the incentives to entrepreneurship markedly weaker, one may expect an undersupply of new firms to be a chronic condition of that economy (see Jensen & Meckling, 1979).

Summing up at this stage, property rights theory clearly suggests that resource allocation is very sensitive to the variance in incentive structures characteristic of each institutional arrangement. Table 5.1, which encapsulates the foregoing considerations, points to privately owned enterprises, and especially to proprietorship (a classical capitalist firm) and joint-stock company (a modern capitalist firm), as superior to non-privately owned enterprises. Actually, the superiority of privately owned enterprises is much

Table 5.1

Problems Involved with Different Forms of Ownership

Form of ownership	Control	Common property	Horizon	Risk diversification	Entry	Problems acknowledged
Private proprietary firm	N	N	Y	Y	N	2
Pnvate partnership	N	Y	Y	N	N	2
Privately owned limited liability company	N	Y	Y	N	N	2
Privately owned joint-stock company	Y	N	N	N	N	1
Publicly owned firm	Y	N	N	Y	Y	3
Labour-managed firm	Y	Y	Y	Y	Y	5
ESOP-type closed firm	N	Y	Y	Y	N	3

The columns Control, Common property, Horizon, Risk diversification, Entry fall under the heading "Type of problem".

[a] Existence of a problem acknowledged in terms of dichotomous Yes/No classification, without measuring intensity of a problem or the impact of the ownership-specific environment on the alleviation or aggravation of a problem.

more marked than the dichotomous classification of Table 5.1 may suggest (the degree of impact of the problem under consideration is not shown there; nor is the ability to cope with the problem within the competitive environment).

The closed-type ESOP firm is a halfway house between the two types of enterprises. Having well defined property rights, it is allocationally more efficient than the publicly owned enterprise and the Yugoslav labour-managed firm. But its characteristic features (strong correlation of employment and ownership; closed character of ownership) reduce its efficiency in comparison with other forms of private ownership.

So far, with one partial exception, I have analysed various institutional arrangements within the framework of the existing market (or, in the Yugoslav case, quasi-market) economy. For the sake of completeness the foregoing real-life arrangements should also be compared with the state-owned enterprise within the framework of a Soviet-type economy. Overwhelming historical arguments apart, comparative economic systems theory posits that on top of the problems of publicly owned enterprises in the market economy, state-owned enterprises in the STE suffer from additional control-related problems of measurement without markets (see, in particular, Szymanderski & Winiecki, 1989; Winiecki, 1991).

Where rewards are dependent on reports to one's superiors rather than on market sales, measurement costs increase enormously. Competition in a market economy sharply reduces measurement costs. Given the incentive structure facing competitive firms, many output manipulations performed by STE enterprises, such as reporting higher output figures than is the case in reality, are plainly impossible. Historically, since the invention of taxation at least, entrepreneurs have been tempted to report less rather than more (to pay lower taxes). Manipulations that are possible, e.g. quality deterioration without commensurate price reduction, are not probable in any time horizon except the short term. Deteriorating consumer opinion, falling sales, profits and accordingly share prices would result in a management shake-up, with or even without takeover, that would put an end to sharp practices of the STE sort.

Without markets, measurement costs rise without limit. The necessary controlling apparatus in theory has to be able to inspect all products in all enterprises in order to compare output volume (planned, reported and actually produced), output structure (planned, reported and actually achieved), quality of inputs (with technological requirements), etc. And all this with respect to millions of products (in the USSR some 20-25 million). These costs are beyond any economy to bear. However, even partial costs are exorbitant. To give an example, in the USSR quality control—and with respect to consumer goods only—employs about 1 million people. Regardless of the army of controllers at all stages, from factory to retail trade, the quality of Soviet consumer goods is certainly abysmally low and may indeed be the lowest in the world (see source quoted in Szymanderski & Winiecki, 1989).

As we can easily see, even if resources are allocated efficiently in an STE (by accident rather than by design, see Winiecki, 1986 and 1988), enterprises may not have the incentives to achieve maximum output. The Jensen & Meckling (1979) thesis quoted at the beginning of this section is more strongly supported in the case of STE enterprises than in any other case. Since the incentive structure induces them, say, simply to write higher output figures into the report rather than to make an actual effort to produce higher output, the availability of resources of the right type, in the right place and at the right time is clearly not enough. Without competitive markets, agency costs in an STE are dramatically higher in the same state-owned enterprises. Thus, on theoretical grounds, STE enterprises can be classified as the particularly inferior institutional arrangement whose inferiority stems from both enterprise-specific and system-specific problems of control. Putting it differently, in STE enterprises shirking in the firm (in Alchian & Demsetz, 1972, terms) takes place alongside shirking by the firm *vis-à-vis* society, i.e. the abstract owner.

Comparative Enterprise and the Social Opportunity Set

Comparative efficiency of alternative (existing) enterprise institutions should not be analysed narrowly within the framework of allocational efficiency associated with output growth, or, in other words, with 'more of the same' (Pejovich, 1987). Wealth can be defined not only in terms of greater quantity of output of the same range of goods and services but also in terms of widening the range of choices (Rosenberg & Birdzell, Jr., 1986) or, in Buchanan's terms of enlarging the social opportunity set (quoted in Pejovich, 1987). One set of institutions may be superior to another not—or not only—because it offers more of the same output, that is, it is more efficient thanks to a better working allocational mechanism, but—or but also—because it creates a more conducive environment for innovation and therefore enlarges the range of choices offered to society.

Here too, as in the case of resource allocation under different institutional arrangements, property rights theory supplies most of the argument. The analytical framework formulated especially by Pejovich (1984, 1987, 1989) is geared to analysis at the comparative economic system level rather than the comparative enterprise level adopted by the present writer in his theoretical case in favour of privatization. At the former level argument in favour of the market system is strongly established.

The *right* to innovate is more widespread in the market system, where everybody is free to engage in innovative activity, than in a Soviet-type economy or Yugoslav labour-managed economy, where multiple restrictions exist in this respect. In an STE workers and managers alike in state-owned enterprises have only the right to suggest this or that innovation, rather than to undertake it. In Yugoslavia collectives of labour-managed firms have the right to innovate, but not individuals within the collective. If somebody has an idea, he or she has to convince the collective as a first step (but this consideration belongs to yet another dimen-

151

sion of comparative analysis, that is the speed of implementation of innovation).

Ability to innovate, another dimension along which Pejovich analyses economic systems, is also more widespread in the market system. Again, anybody with a good idea can obtain resources on the financial markets at a price that reflects market evaluation of its prospects (including the riskiness of an innovation). In an STE resources are allocated by or at the decision of the centre at below market price, in the form of subsidy or low-interest loan, and they are obtainable only by authorised managers of state-owned enterprises—and by nobody else. The situation in Yugoslavia is different but not much better in this respect; the employees' collective in a labour-managed firm has not only the right but also the ability to apply for financial resources. However, this ability is strongly circumscribed by the nature of the labour-managed firm. The incentives structure in such a firm leaves a very small part of profits for further expansion, be it through investment or investment cum innovation (see the preceding section). This makes the banking system almost the sole source of funds for innovation—in contrast to undistributed profits, issue of share and/or bonds, recourse to venture capital institutions plus the banking system in the capitalist market economy. Worse still, banks in Yugoslavia are owned by local governments and enterprises, with the latter being their largest borrowers. Under the circumstances bank loans are allocated not in accordance with the profitability principle (including the riskiness of a loan) but with the interests of the founders. These interests and the prospective benefits of innovation do not necessarily coincide, especially under the conditions of assured survival of labour-managed firms.

The argument for privatisation at the enterprise level begins in Pejovich's classification with the incentives to innovate for all ownership forms in the market economy environment. These are the strongest for the owner of a proprietary firm who has the right to the residual income and, consequently, has the strongest incentive to turn the idea (his own or anybody else's) into a product or process. Partnerships and limited liability companies fare as well as proprietorships, given the well assigned rights to the residual income.

The situation of a joint-stock company is somewhat different, given the dispersed ownership and its separation from management. Here, however, the impact of competitive markets reinforces the incentives for managers. A manager captures benefits of successful innovation in two ways. In the short run he receives a reward (bonus) for improving the profitability of his company. In the longer run he enhances his prospects for promotion because the stock market constantly evaluates enterprises through share price changes and these signals are used in the market for managers. Improved profitability translates itself into higher share prices and these, in turn, into a higher evaluation of a successful manager.

Not only positive incentives are at work in the case of managers of joint-stock companies but also negative ones. Continuous low profitability that may stem from preference for routine, a quiet life, or leisure on the job are translated into low share prices that increase the probability of takeover—and loss of job for the manager. Moreover, the opportunities of the market for managers may under such circumstances turn into a threat as well. For not only may the manager's present job be in jeopardy but so may similarly well paid future jobs. Thus, the correlation of incentive structure and well functioning markets (stock market, market for managers, market for takeovers) makes the joint-stock company an efficient institution in furthering innovation.

This, however, is not the case with a publicly owned enterprise. Managers have less incentive to innovate than they have to invest in the expansion of their enterprise. The latter at least gives them the opportunity to become managers of a bigger firm and, accordingly, to improve both status and income. The former need not require larger size and therefore the manager's benefits from innovation may be less than the countervailing benefits of routine, a quiet life, or leisure on the job. Furthermore, as bureaucratic appointees, managers of publicly owned enterprises neither capture benefits from the market for managers nor face a threat from the market for takeovers.

Those who represent an abstract owner—politicians and bureaucrats—may themselves be interested in innovation. This interest, however, need not be related to expected increase in profitability. 'Technological progress' (in other words: prestige) may be an important goal in the non-market-based push for innovation. Such innovation may actually decrease profitability, as the experience not only of state enterprises in STEs but also that of SOEs in the West testifies. Thence stem many 'white elephants' of the Concorde type.

The labour-managed firm is in no better situation in this respect. Just as in the case of investment (see the preceding section), an employee has to convince his fellow co-workers and/or workers' council on the benefits that innovation is expected to bring. Simultaneously, he is conscious of the fact that regardless of his efforts he or she will reap only $1/N$ of the prospective reward (with N being equal to the number of employees in the firm). The rule that it is only a collective that has both the right and the ability to innovate creates a common property problem and significantly reduces incentives to innovate.

However, this is not the end of the disincentives that beset a labour-managed firm. The structure of property rights affects both the length of life and the type of innovation acceptable for a labour-managed firm. With respect to the former, employees' time horizon makes more acceptable those innovations whose pay-off period is no longer than the expected period of employment of the majority of employees deciding on the issue. This excludes a category of innovations that may increase the present value of the firm but, given their life span, will not be acceptable. In turn, with respect to the latter, certain types of innovation, e.g. those that may decrease income per employee, will not be acceptable either.

It is worth noting that a manager in a labour-managed firm who is appointed by a workers' council also has weaker incentives to

154

innovate than his counterpart in a privately owned firm. He is not able to capture the benefits of innovation on the market for managers. His prospective advancement in salary in a given firm or appointment to a better paid managerial position in another firm is not dependent on the track record of the share prices on the stock market because such a record does not exist. A Yugoslav type labour-managed firm does not have well assigned, partitioned and transferable property rights. Moreover, as his position depends on the votes of the collective, he has to adjust his own preferences to the preferences of those who keep him in his position. All this makes a labour-managed firm a weak competitor as far as innovation is concerned.

In a closed-type ESOP firm well assigned property rights create incentives for owner-employees to innovate which by and large are comparable to those in private partnerships and limited liability companies. Employees are able to capture benefits of innovation through shareholding after termination of employment (including retirement). However, certain types of innovation will not be acceptable, especially those that sharply reduce employment (see the preceding section's comment on incentives to invest).

At the same time managers in these firms do not fully capture benefits of innovation on the market for managers since a closed-type ESOP firm is not publicly quoted and therefore their track record as managers is not as well documented as that of managers of privately owned joint-stock companies. Furthermore, just like managers of labour-managed firms, they have to adjust to the incentive structure of owner-employees. Therefore, they too are willing to press for a narrower range of innovations than managers of other privately owned firms in order not to come into collision with the owner-employees.

To the foregoing, yet another dimension of the comparative analysis of innovation could be added, that is social evaluation of innovation. This, too, is applicable only at the comparative systems level. The private property-based capitalist market system is definitely superior in this respect *vis-à-vis* its alternatives. As stressed by Pelikan (1985), the capitalist system separates those who market innovation (product or process) from both those who are asked to finance innovation and those who decide whether to buy it. As a result, in the capitalist market economy there is much less adherence to erroneous innovation decisions than in any systemic alternative, where this separation is either incomplete (in a Yugoslav labour-managed economy) or does not exist at all (in a Soviet-type economy). For the same reasons it is also superior to a hypothetical SOE-based market economy, that is to 'market socialism'.

Summing up, the market system is, at the comparative systems level of analysis, clearly superior to any non-market one with respect to enlarging the social opportunity set through innovation. Furthermore, at the comparative enterprise level privately owned firms have stronger incentives to innovate. Thus, it is not just any market economy but a capitalist market economy, where privately owned firms dominate, that is superior to any alternative institutional arrangement in this particular respect.

Comparative Enterprise and the State

Enterprises of different ownership form within the market system may also be compared along yet another dimension, that is, the impact of the state, as represented by politicians and bureaucrats, on its performance. The impact is not invariant with regard to ownership form of the enterprise. Let it be added that nor is it invariant with regard to economic system at another level of comparative analysis (a point that will be taken up towards the end of this section). It is, however, comparative enterprise that is of primary interest here.

The analysis in question may be pursued using three different types of argument, each derived from a different strand of economic theory. The first type of argument comes, like most of the

156

arguments so far, from property rights theory. It concerns weaker incentives to seek effficient outcomes. As stressed already at the beginning, state decision makers, be they politicians or bureaucrats, do not own the resources they control and, consequently, they neither appropriate the full benefits from their decisions nor bear their full cost (Pejovich, 1990). Thus, the penalty/reward structure is not conducive to efficient outcomes.

Important theoretical implications for comparative enterprise stem from this conclusion. The larger the share of resources used for productive purposes that remains in the hands of the state (i.e. is distributed through a political resource allocation process), the higher will be the fraction of the total that will be used inefficiently. It is obvious that the SOE or publicly owned enterprise receives a much larger fraction of its resources through a political resource allocation process than does the privately owned enterprise (regardless of ownership form of the latter). This fact by itself puts the former at a disadvantage *vis-à-vis* the latter as far as efficiency is concerned.

The labour-managed firm or closed ESOP firm, that halfway house between labour-managed and privately owned firms, is much less affected than the SOE. However, to the extent that they enjoy preferential treatment they may (and in the case of ESOPs they do) benefit from tax relief of one sort or another. This in itself may somewhat weaken incentives to evaluate carefully the impact of their activities upon the present value of their firm.

I am conscious of the fact that I may be seen as biased in my assessment since I do not admit the possibility of greater efficiency of a political resource allocation process *vis-à-vis* a market-based one. Although refuted historically, this argument will none the less be dealt with theoretically later on.

The second type of argument concerns not so much weaker incentives to seek efficient outcomes, i.e. those increasing the present value of the future stream of profits from successful ventures, but probable strong incentives for both politicians and bureaucrats to pursue activities and seek outcomes that promote their own interests rather than those of the general public. These arguments come from public choice theory, whose protagonists have long argued that there is a need to apply a uniform analytical framework to all types of resource allocation. Both private and public economy are inhabited by the same human beings, with varied motives and interests. The dichotomy of the private economy with its economic agents driven by egoistic and narrowly individualistic interests and the public economy managed by disinterested politicians and bureaucrats solely motivated by public interest is a myth (for an early formulation of the arguments, see Buchanan & Tollison, 1972). In such a world 'government failure' is at least as probable as 'market failure', quite apart from problems of property rights of politicians and bureaucrats or their omniscience.

In fact, public choice theorists stress that the probability of government failure, owing to the diversion of resources to other uses than those efficiently satisfying public interest, is much stronger. This is not intended to mean that politicians or bureaucrats are characterised by lower standards of professionalism, or work ethics or honesty but by what Gordon Tullock calls 'institution constraints' (Tullock, 1965 and 1976). The rules of the game that determine individual behaviour are far more rigorous in private firms than in the world of politics or bureaucracy. In the latter individuals have greater opportunity to give free rein to their individual interests, regardless of their relationship to the interests of the general public.

Some authors close to—but not identical with—the public choice school stress that the rules of the game create looser constraints generally not by design but owing to the indivisibilities in the output of the political process and that of public administration (see, e.g. Olson, 1965, 1973 and 1986). It is self-evident, however, that these characteristics of political resource allocation suggest that, given the more stringent constraints on individual behaviour in private firms, allocation of resources for goods and services where indivisibilities do not arise is better left to the privately owned enterprise.

There are clear-cut implications from the foregoing for the analysis of comparative enterprise. Also, these implications reinforce conclusions supplied by property rights theory. Given the motives and interests of bureaucrats and politicians, the publicly owned enterprise is expected to behave with lesser care for the best use of resources it receives. For not only may politicians and bureaucrats, who have no property rights to residual profits, allocate resources to a publicly owned enterprise without due concern for the present value of the future stream of profits resulting from investing the resources in question, but they may also have their personal motives and objectives in allocating these resources in a plainly inefficient manner (see the preceding section's example of prestigeous projects of the 'Concorde' type).

Again, although all enterprises, privately owned, labour-managed or publicly owned, may compete for resources allocated through a political process, the threat of inefficient outcome is the strongest for those whose prospects for being bailed out in the case of financial failure are greatest. Paraphrasing a well known bankers' saying, politicians and bureaucrats may have greater propensity to throw one bundle of bad money after another in the case of the latter enterprise. Not only is the budget constraint made softer (in the Kornai, 1979, sense) in the latter enterprise as a result, but also its acceptance by the management may be more welcome owing to different incentive structures for managers in privately and publicly owned enterprises.

Management in the former has to face the possibility of a more or less sudden termination of the inflow of politically allocated resources (in consequence of political change or unexpectedly deep recession that reduces the degree of freedom in political resource allocation). Financial decline of a private firm will adversely affect the evaluation of its managers on the market for managerial talent. In contrast, managers of publicly owned enterprises are more often than not appointed on the basis of different criteria (political loyalty, seniority in public service, etc.). Therefore they are less concerned about efficient outcomes of activities of the firm they manage at a given moment.

While analyzing the motives and interests of politicians and bureaucrats yet another type of political interference in publicly owned enterprise should be taken into account. One cannot exclude the misuse of a publicly owned enterprise's behaviour for partisan purposes. Given the dispersed property rights across the whole population of a country (or a locality), politicians may raise the question of the propriety of a given course of action taken by publicly owned enterprise(s) to suit their political goals of scoring points against the party in power. The general absence of objective criteria for judging the efficiency of outcomes of alternative strategies may facilitate the creation of a wave of indignation of dispersed owners who will protest—and later vote—against the government in power.

What I have in mind here is the unnecessary constraints that are put on managers of publicly owned enterprises with respect to their range of choice in fulfilling their managerial duties. An example of such abuse of the political process and its impact on managers' behaviour may be in order here. The well known management consultant Tom Peters (1990) describes innovative strategies of various firms. Some of them deliberately increase pressure on themselves to continue to be innovative: for example, Quad/Graphics, a fast-growing, high-technology printing firm, sells everything it develops to every customer, including rival firms. In this way the owner-manager 'purposefully keeps the heat turned up under himself' (Peters, 1990, p. 10). Peters offers many more similar examples. Now for the sake of argument let us assume that a publicly owned firm which spent a lot of state money on R&D did the same. Who could guarantee that its management would not face the charge of 'wasting taxpayers money' or outright corruption ('selling out its comparative advantage')? In complicated matters of non-routine entrepreneurial/managerial decisions, managers of publicly owned enterprises are at an obvious disadvantage.

Finally, yet another type of argument should be used in analysing comparative enterprise and the state. It is the Hayekian knowledge problem (for the best presentation thereof, see Lavoie, 1985). It runs as follows. In the traditional approach to knowledge, knowledge is objective, quantitative and cumulative. In the limit, objective knowledge can conceivably become complete. The growth-of-knowledge school of the philosophy of science rejects that view. Knowledge, in the view of Michael Polanyi and Friedrich von Hayek, is a spontaneous outcome of the skilled performance of scientists who interact among themselves. Knowledge is qualitative, as well as quantitative, and it enhances our tacit understanding of reality. As we learn more, we discover new questions whose existence we did not suspect before. Therefore, it is integrative rather than cumulative. In the pursuit of knowledge scientists are called upon continuously to make tacit judgements that are not completely specified in their theories or formal models but which are indispensable in the quest for knowledge. Tacit knowledge underlies all articulated knowledge.

This tacit dimension is extremely important because it is evidence of the inarticulability or incommunicability of a large part of an individual scientist's knowledge about a given aspect of the observed reality. Now, if the rigorous quest for knowledge is so heavily dependent on tacit knowledge of individual members of the scientific community, this is, as Lavoie (1985) rightly points out, all the more true about the kind of knowledge that is relevant to economic decision making.

Knowledge concerning business decisions is dispersed among hundreds thousands of owners, owner-managers and professional managers of all levels. It is to a large extent knowledge of particular circumstances that cannot be fully communicated to one's superiors. This decentralised, local, partly tacit knowledge is, however, revealed in their actions. Encapsulated in market prices, it creates in the market system a tendency for adjustment (although at any moment some economic agents may be in disequilibrium). In this way, as Lavoie—following sociobiologists—puts it, the 'social intelligence' of the market is greater than that of its constituent parts, that is economic agents.

At this point we have arrived at the (allegedly neglected) issue of possible superiority of political over market-based allocation of resources. The growth-of-knowledge philosophy of science supplies the most devastating argument in the market-versus-plan debate. Given the tacitness and locally bounded nature of a large part of the knowledge necessary for business decisions, central planners (or 'the state') are doomed to have a dramatically lower knowledge input. Since tacit knowledge is incommunicable, central planners are forced to depend on their own intelligence (plus that of their advisers), and the Hayekian process of competitive discovery through market prices, encapsulating effects of decisions based on otherwise inarticulated tacit knowledge, is lost. Individual intelligence, not the infinitely higher social intelligence achieved through the market system, is the rule under the plan.

The Austrian school's critique of central planning is crucial for the comparative systems level of analysis. However, the line of reasoning based on tacit, locally bounded knowledge of economic agents may be easily extended to the comparative enterprise level. Thus, politicians and bureaucrats who participate in political allocation of resources not only have weaker incentives to seek efficient outcomes and may be motivated to seek outcomes that are not necessarily in accordance with the goal of efficiency. They also have a lower knowledge input into the decision-making process than economic agents interacting among themselves. (Incidentally, this is also an argument against picking winners, that is industrial targeting; see Eliasson, 1987.)

It may be said that the more disaggregated the target, the greater the disadvantage of political resource allocation owing to the lower knowledge input. Thus, economy-wide decisions are less disadvantaged in this respect than enterprise-specific ones. The implications for publicly owned enterprise are unequivocal— and positively correlated with earlier arguments. All theories referred to in this section (property rights, public choice and Austrian school) suggest that privately owned enterprise leaves less room for allocational decisions whose outcomes are hindered by a variety of motivation-based and knowledge-based inefficiencies.

In sum, whatever aspect of wealth creating capability we examine, be it efficiency of resource allocation, innovation or impact of the state upon wealth creation, private enterprise emerges as a superior solution *within* the framework of the market system. Economic theory no less than economic history proves the superiority of private enterprise, and argument in favour of private enterprise is eo ipso an argument in favour of privatisation of SOEs in a post-Soviet-type economy.

References

Alchian, A.A. & Demsetz, H. (1972), 'Production, Information Costs and Economic Organiztion', *American Economic Review*, 62, 5.

Alessi, L. de (1982), 'On the Nature and Consequences of Private and Public Enterprise', *Minnesota Law Review*, 67, 1.

Berle, Jr., A.A. & Means, G.C. (1932), *The Modern Corporation and Private Property*, Macmillan, New York.

Buchanan, J.M. & Tollison, R.D., eds. (1972), *Theory of Public Choice: Political Applications of Economics*, University of Michigan Press, Ann Arbor, MI.

Demsetz, H. (1969), 'Information and Efficiency: Another Viewpoint', *Journal of Law and Economics*, 12, 1.

Eggertsson, T. (1990), *Economic Behaviour and Institutions*, Cambridge University Press, Cambridge.

Eliasson, G. (1987), *Technological Competition and Trade in the Experimentally Organized Economy*, Research Report No. 32, Industrial Institute for Economic and Social Research, Stockholm.

Elliot, J.E. (1973), *Comparative Economic Systems*, Prentice-Hall, Englewood Cliffs, NJ.

Fama, E.F. & Jensen, M.C. (1985), 'Organizational Forms and Investment Decisions', *Journal of Financial Economics*, 14, 1.

Furubotn, E. (1976), 'The Long-Run Analysis of the Labor-Managed Firm', *American Economic Review*, 66, pp. 104-123.

Furubotn, E. & Pejovich, S. (1972), 'Property Rights and Economic Theory: A Survey of Recent Literature', *Journal of Economic Literature*, 10, December, pp. 1137-1162.

Furubotn, E. & Pejovich, S. (1974), 'Property Rights and the Behavior of the Firm in a Socialist State: The Example of Yugoslavia', in: Furubotn, E. & Pejovich, S. eds., *The Economics of Property Rights*, Ballinger, Cambridge, MA.

Hayek, F. von [1935], 'The Present State of the Debate', reprinted (1948) in: *Individualism and World Order*, University of Chicago Press, Chicago.

Hayek, F. von (1945), 'The Use of Knowledge in Society', *American Economic Review*, 35, pp. 519-530.

Heimann, E. (1922), *Mehrwert und Gemeinwirtschaft: Kritische und positive Beitraege zur Theorie des Sozialismus*, Robert Engelmann, Berlin.

Jensen, M.C. & Meckling, W.J. (1976), 'Theory of the Firm: Managerial Behavior, Agency Costs and Ownership Structure', *Journal of Financial Economics*, 3, 4.

Jensen, M.C. & Meckling, W.J. (1979), 'Rights and Production Functions: An Application to Labor-Managed Firms and Codetermination', *Journal of Business*, 52, 4.

Kornai, J. (1979), 'Resource-Constrained versus Demand-Constrained Systems', *Econometrica*, 47, 4.

Lavoie, D. (1985a), *Rivalry and Central Planning: The Socialist Calculation Debate Reconsidered*, Cambridge University Press, Cambridge.

Lavoie, D. (1985), *National Economic Planning: What Is Left?*, Ballinger, Cambridge, MA.

Mises, L. von (1923), 'Neue Beitraege zum Problem der sozialistischen Wirtschaftsrechnung', *Archiv fuer Sozialwissenschaft und Sozialpolitik*, 51, pp. 488-500. (Translated and published in 1936 as an appendix to *Socialism ...*, see below.)

Mises, L. von (1936), *Socialism: An Economic and Sociological Analysis*, Jonathan Cape, London.

Mises, L. von (1949), *Human Action: A Treatise on Economics*, William Holge, London.

Olson, M. (1965), *The Logic of Collective Action: Public Goods and a Theory of Groups*, Harvard University Press, Cambridge, MA.

Olson, M. (1973), 'Evaluating Performance in the Public Sector', in: M. Moss, ed., *The Measurement of Economic and Social Performance*, Studies in Income and Wealth, Vol. 38, Columbia University Press, New York.

Olson, M. (1986), 'Toward a More General Theory of Governmental Structure', *American Economic Review*, 76, May, pp. 120-125.

Pejovich, S. (1984), 'The Incentives to Innovate Under Alternative Property Rights', *Cato Journal*, pp. 427-446.

Pejovich, S. (1987), 'Freedom, Property Rights and Innovation in Socialism', *Kyklos*, 40, Fasc. 4.

Pejovich, S. (1989), *A Property Rights Analysis of the Yugoslav 'Miracle'*, Center for Free Enterprise, Texas A&M University mimeo.

Pejovich, S. (1990), *The Economics of Property Rights: Toward a Theory of Comparative Systems*, Kluwer, Dordrecht.

Pelikan, P. (1985), Private Enterprise vs. Government Control: An Organizationally Dynamic Comparison, The Industrial Institute for Economic and Social Research, Stockholm, Working Paper, mimeo, January.

Peters, T. (1990), 'Get Innovative or Get Dead', *California Management Review*, 33, 1, Fall.

Pryke, R.S. (1971), *Public Enterprise in Practice*, MacGibbon & Kee, London.

Pryke, R.S. (1981), *The Nationalised Industries. Policies and Performance since 1968*, MacGibbon & Kee, London.

Robbins, L. (1934), *The Great Depression*, Macmillan, New York.

Rosenberg, N. & Birdzell, Jr., L.E., *How the West Grew Rich. The Economic Transformation of the Industrial World*, Basic Books, New York.

Shonfield, A. (1965), *Modern Capitalism: The Changing Balance of Private and Public Power*, Oxford University Press, London..

Szymanderski, J. & Winiecki, J. (1989), 'Dissipation de la rente, managers et travailleurs dans le systeme sovietique: les implications pour un changement du systeme', *Revue d'etudes comparatives Est-Ouest*, 20, 1, pp. 566-589.

Tullock, G. (1965), *The Politics of Bureaucracy*, Public Affairs Press, Washington, DC.

Tullock, G., ed. (1976), *The Vote Motive*, Institute of Economic Affairs, London.

Ward, B. (1958), 'The Firm in Illyria: Market Syndicalism', *American Economic Review*, 48, September, pp. 566-589.

Winiecki, J. (1986), 'Distorted Macroeconomics of Central Planning', *Banca Nazionale del Lavoro Quarterly Review*, 157, June.

Winiecki, J. (1988), *The Distorted World of Soviet-Type Economies*, Routledge, London.

Winiecki, J. (1991), *Resistance to change in the Soviet Economic System. Property Rights Approach*, Routledge, London.

6 Privatization primer: Avoiding major mistakes

Economic theory tells us that of the various forms of ownership, private ownership is the most efficient. But theory tells little about how to get from where East-Central Europe is at present to an economy with predominantly private ownership. The ongoing privatisation debates reflect uncertainty regarding the proper paths to privatisation, as well as conflicting goals and interests. Goals, paths and interests are, in fact, interrelated, adding to the complexity of the problem.

In recognition of this complexity, this paper will not offer yet another allegedly guaranteed formula for success. It is, rather, a (probably non-comprehensive) list of major mistakes that can be made with respect to privatization coupled with recommendations on how to avoid them. The existence of some trade-offs among potential mistakes, however, implies that not all of them can be completely avoided.

The relative success of the East-Central European countries in avoiding these mistakes will be evaluated. The paper deals only with the post-communist economies of the region. East Germany is excluded from comparative evaluation for obvious reasons, while Yugoslavia is included (even if it does not fit exactly the 'post-communist' formula at the federal level).

Avoiding 'Capitalism Without Capitalists'

One of the pitfalls on the path to a capitalist market economy is associated with the muddle over the relationship between private property and the market. The muddle is ideological in its origins. The democratic left is now ready to accept the market (see Le Grand & Estrin, 1989). In fact, after the collapse of state planning, it has little choice!

However, a corollary of the market economy is private ownership (for critiques of market socialism, see Baechler, 1980 and de Jasay, 1990). But left-leaning economists, not being able to accept both market and private ownership at the same time, have been busy for some time devising various schemes aimed at the creation of 'capitalism without capitalists' (Winiecki, 1990a).

Although these ideas originate mostly in the West, some of their protagonists have found adherents within East-Central European governments and major political groups. The most fashionable of these illusion-spinning schemes are state holding companies, or state investment banks, or 'state-somethings' that are to be allocated a majority of shares in state enterprises turned into joint-stock companies (see Gomulka, 1989; Nuti, 1988 and 1989; Iwanek & Swiecicki, 1987; and Swiecicki, 1988). Bureaucratically appointed managers of such institutions would then be expected to simulate the behaviour of managers in privately owned firms in the stock market. They would be given the same rights as shareholders, except that they would not benefit from capital gains or pay the price of capital losses.

At the level of interaction between the state bureaucracy and state enterprise managers, these schemes can be criticised in terms of public choice theory. Politicians and bureaucrats are not impartial umpires deciding on the issues in a disinterested manner. They have their own interests (re-election for the former, empire-building and/or leisure on the job for the latter) which influence their relations with state enterprise managers.

It is an illusion to expect that 'playing at the stock market game' may be more important for both sides of the interaction than these other interests. Walters & Monsen concluded in their 1983 study of West European state enterprises that they had 'not been able to discover a single case of a top executive of a European nationalized company who was replaced for failing to earn a required rate of financial return. By contrast, there are dozens of cases of managers who have resigned in protest, been fired, or were not reappointed because of a major disagreement with their governments over policy'.

At the level of conflict of interest between owner (the state) and manager, illusions of 'capitalism without capitalists' can be criticised in terms of property rights and agency theory. Private ownership links investment decisions to capital gains and losses and is thus more efficient than state ownership, which offers much more room for opportunistic behaviour on the part of managers.

There is a world of difference between the shareholder who uses his own knowledge or hires a specialist to play the stock market with his own money and a bureaucrat who risks the state's (i.e. taxpayer's) money. As Kornai (1990) aptly points out, 'simulated joint-stock companies, the simulated capital market, and the simulated stock-exchange' all 'add up to ... Wall Street—all made of plastic'.

All of the East-Central European post-communist countries have resisted the temptation to go for a fake rather than a genuine article. In this resistance they have shown greater maturity than some of their Western advisers. Not all of them, however, have avoided another ideological trap, namely that of a 'third road' in the form of self-managed (or labour managed) firms and their more recent successor, employee share ownership (see the critique in Gruszecki & Winiecki, 1991).

These illusions have been strongest—not surprisingly—in Yugoslavia, where it was planned to sell up to 60% of shares value to employees in each enterprise. The non-transferability of shares was to be introduced for an unspecified period. Employee-owned firms of that sort are only marginally better in efficiency terms than labour-managed firms (Gruszecki & Winiecki, 1990). Their successes, alleged or real, should be seen in the context of the market dominance of privately-owned firms that force efficient behaviour on employee-owned firms.

If employee-owned firms become the dominant form of ownership, however, their deficiencies known from property rights and agency theory will leave a strong imprint upon their performance—and on that of the economy as a whole. In Yugoslavia all 'third road' attempts stem also from the interest of the communist ruling elite in perpetuating themselves in power. They are also increasingly perceived as a vehicle of Serbian domination over the more capitalist-oriented northern republics of Slovenia and Croatia.

In Poland, however, a lobby in favour of self-management in the recent past and of employee share ownership currently is strongly linked to the victorious Solidarity, unfortunately giving these concepts enhanced credibility. The Polish government has wisely resisted attempts at making either of these ideas a dominant form of denationalization, but the pressure continues to be strong. Hungary is the country where these 'third road' illusions are weakest.

Three Most Damaging Mistakes

There are many ways in which privatization could go wrong, quite apart from opting for 'capitalism without capitalists' or some 'third road'. Three errors, in particular, are likely to be the most damaging for successful privatization, namely: (1) concentrating upon the means or methods of privatization before considering its goals; (2) neglecting the time factor; and (3) disregarding the politics of privatisation.

Some countries, lured by the glamour of the British-style privatisation through public sale of shares of enterprises, have concentrated on this particular method to the detriment of clear thinking about what they want to achieve. If the goal were 'people's capitalism' (with as wide a dispersion of ownership as possible), then British-style privatization would be a conceivable means to achieve it. But the United Kingdom already had a well-established capitalist class, while the East-Central European countries do not. Since the kernel of the capitalist market system is, not surprisingly, capitalists—people who take capital risk—the transition to the capitalist market economy should entail measures that support the emergence of capitalists.

A sale of small lots of shares to the general public is not helpful in this respect. At least some other means, such as sale of small and medium-sized enterprises to private individuals or small groups of individuals, or sale to foreigners of some enterprises or controlling blocks of shares should also be considered.

The first Polist non-communist government gave its highest priority to designing the rules for British-style privatization. But the not unexpected result was that it had continuously to scale down its public sale-based privatisation plans, from 150 enterprises in 1990 to 50 and, finally, to 5 enterprises privatized in January 1991. At that rate privatization would last several hundred years. Privatisation of commercial real property (shops, restaurants, pharmacies, etc.) is proceeding at varying speed in different areas, while the sale of small state-owned enterprises has not really even begun.

Hungary did not completely avoid the lure of the tried and tested British-style privatisation. However, the government has understood well the need to foster a domestic capitalist class, and has, therefore, been more active in selling small and medium-sized enterprises to domestic entrepreneurs. At the same time, it also has understood the need for ownership control over management and is generally concerned about finding buyers of a controlling block of shares.

Czecho-Slovakia, a late starter, has followed a markedly different privatization path, particularly with regard to larger state-owned enterprises. It began the process of selling off small state enterprises and commercial property in early 1991. Yugoslavia, with its unfinished political change and communist influence, has given a high priority in its privatization programme to the conversion from labour-managed firms to employee share ownership.

The second major mistake is to forget that various methods of privatization require differing time spans for implementation—and time is a scarce commodity for countries in transition to the market system. A propensity for state enterprise managers to overinvest and generally use more resources in times of expansionary macroeconomic policy is well known. An economy with predominantly state ownership is unbalanced by definition, and is also inflation prone. (Recent Polish experience showed that in times of restrictive macroeconomic policy, such an economy is unbalanced and recession prone; see Winiecki, 1990b.) Accordingly, privatization should proceed rapidly to change the highly unsatisfactory ownership structure in favour of privately owned firms.

It is here that the British-style privatisation reveals its major weakness in the East-Central European context. Asset valuation, preparation of prospectuses for would-be buyers, advertising campaigns and, finally, public subscription all require time. The privatisation of one or two dozen enterprises in the United Kingdom took more than a decade.

Could the East Central European countries, with their thousands of state enterprises, not to mention their rudimentary financial markets, follow the pattern? After persisting in this illusion for some time, the Polish government (both the Mazowiecki and the Bielecki one) began to search for more rapid means of privatization that could be applied in parallel with public sales of shares. Czecho-Slovakia recognised from the start that public sales could last for decades, if not centuries, and opted for a free (or almost free—there are nominal charges only) distribution of a large part of state industrial assets to its citizens according to a voucher scheme entitling them to receive shares in enterprises of their own choice up to the value of the voucher. Only Hungary has stuck to the idea of the 'businesslike' (i.e., sale only) privatization that may last for decades.

Kornai (1990) has cautioned that *embourgeoisement* is a long process and has warned against 'instituting private property by a cavalry attack'. However, an acceleration of this process should not be regarded as impossible (see Beksiak, Gruszecki, Jedraszczyk & Winiecki, 1989; see also Gruszecki & Winiecki, 1991). If the alternative is half a century to a century of privatization, shortcut privatization is not only possible but also highly desirable. The costs of decades of dominance of state ownership will certainly be higher than those resulting from unavoidable problems associated with the free distribution of state assets to citizens. Quite a few analysts in East-Central Europe and elsewhere have agreed with this conclusion.

The last major mistake to be considered concerns the neglect of building a political constituency for privatization. After all, it is a major political change and, as such, coalitions supporting the change are needed. 'People's capitalism', the spreading widely of the ownership of financial assets, is an approach that may under proper circumstances (as in the United Kingdom, for example), receive wide acceptance. However, the impoverished populations of the post-communist countries are clearly unable to buy, even at discounted prices, the bulk of state industrial assets.

Therefore, free distribution to the population is preferable for reasons of both political efficacy and equity. Free distribution would generate more political support than sale, which would give too large a share to the hated communist *nomenklatura.*

Political efficacy considerations suggest yet another rationale for free distribution of state assets to the population. The population at large may be the only constituency that can be organized to resist the claims of a less numerous but already better organized constituency: employees of large state-owned enterprises who prefer the free distribution of assets to employees over distribution to the population at large.

The previous Polish government failed to recognise the importance of building a political constituency, although its single-
minded pursuit of British-style privatization did not give it much
of a chance to find one. Hungary fares better only because employee ownership is not so popular there, but the insistence on the
sale of assets rather than free distribution limits grass roots support for privatization. Czecho-Slovakia, with its free distribution
scheme, seems to have generated greater popular support for privatization. In Yugoslavia, the idea of selling rather than giving
shares in enterprises to their employees did not win much enthusiasm. Workers were already receiving the benefits of ownership
without having to pay for the shares.

Summing up, when it comes to avoiding the most damaging
mistakes, Czecho-Slovakia is clearly in the lead, with Hungary
next, Poland coming a poor third, and Yugoslavia bringing up the
rear. Not only had Yugoslavia made all three mistakes discussed
here (as has Poland to some extent), but it is on an altogether
wrong track—an as yet incompletely defined 'third road'.

One caveat is necessary at this point. It is not possible to avoid
all mistakes simultaneously. For example, if Czecho-Slovakia de-
cides to speed up the privatization process by the free distribution
of a large part of state industrial assets (through the voucher
scheme), then it will privatize sooner than other post-communist
countries in East-Central Europe. Most probably, the privatization
will also be smoother thanks to greater political support. But this
choice entails costs as well as benefits. Free distribution leads to
large dispersion of ownership with all the attendant costs of
weaker control by owners over managers. Although it is expected
that the process of reconcentration would start soon, the interim
period would be one of weaker performance than under traditional
capitalist control with clearly identifiable owners of the controlling block of shares. To lower these unavoidable costs somewhat,
the privatization should envisage a mix of methods. A combination of free distribution of assets to citizens could be combined,
for example, with a small scale (10-20%) free distribution of

shares to employees. This combination would create the clearly identifiable group of owners right from the start. Of course, there are disadvantages to even temporary employee control: shares would not be concentrated in the hands of a group willing to effect radical change in the organisation.

On Not Putting All the Eggs in One Basket

The last issue to be considered is the choice of the one and only versus that of many methods of privatization. Given the fact that the road to success is unknown, a simultaneous application of a broad array of privatization approaches is another insurance against failure. Sale of small and middle-sized enterprises to individuals, sale of some larger firms to foreigners, free distribution of shares in most larger firms to citizens—all these are complementary rather than competing solutions. Those countries employing simultaneously a variety of approaches stand a better change of success. Hungary appears to be in the lead in this respect, with Poland ahead of Czecho-Slovakia (perhaps owing to the head start of the transition in Poland).

While considering a broad array of privatisation approaches as an insurance against failure under high uncertainty, yet another issue should be noted. The analysis here has focused on what Gruszecki & Winiecki (1991) call 'privatization from above', or the reassignment of property rights of the formerly state-owned enterprises. On the other hand, the success of the change in the ownership structure of post-communist economies depends also on 'privatization from below', that is, on the unfettered establishment and expansion of private firms.

These considerations of not putting all the eggs in one basket would be incomplete without mentioning the demand for the creation of a network of market institutions attuned to the needs of the expanding private sector (at this stage, composed almost exclusively of small businesses). Small business development banks, agricultural development banks, small business-oriented insurance companies, innovation centres and venture capital institutions are urgently needed as ingredients for success.

There is a bias in governments' efforts in favour of the more glamorous aspects of institution-building: establishment of the two-tier banking system, privatization of large state enterprises, and the establishment of a stock market. But small businesses, whether privatized or built by their owners from scratch, all critically depend for their expansion on a network of institutions that in no post-communst economy are yet in place, even in a rudimentary state. The deficiencies of these institutions are so great in all of the countries in question that no ranking of nations is even possible.

Regardless of ranking, however, difficulties are enormous everywhere and many things may happen in East-Central Europe on the way to the future. We do not know all the answers and paths leading from here to there. And let us not forget that 'there', meaning the West, is a moving—not a static—target.

References

Baechler, J. (1990), 'Liberty, Property, and Equality', *Nomos*, Vol. 2, pp. 269-288.

Beksiak, J., Gruszecki, T., Jedraszczyk, A. & Winiecki, J. (1989), 'Outline of a Programme for Stabilisation and Systemic Change', published in English (1990) in *The Polish Transformation: Programme and Progress*, Centre for Research into Communist Economies, London.

Gomulka, S. (1989), 'How to Create a Capital Market in a Socialist Country, and How to Use it for the Purpose of Changing the System of Ownership'. Prepared for the LSE Financial Markets Group Conference on 'New Financial Markets: Economic Reform in Eastern Europe', 13 December, mimeo.

Gruszecki, T. (1991), 'Privatization in Poland in 1990', *Communist Economies and Economic Transformation*, Vol. 3, No. 2, pp. 141-154.

Gruszecki, T. & Winiecki, J. (1991), 'Privatization in East-Central Europe: A Comparative Perspective', *Aussenwirtschaft*, No. 1.

Iwanek, M. & Swiecicki, M. (1987), 'Handlowac Kapitalem w Socjalizmie' (How to Trade With Capital Under Socialism), *Polityka*, 16 June.

Jasay, A. de (1990), 'Market Socialism: A Scrutiny - This Square Circle', Institute of Economic Affairs Occasional Paper 84, London.

Kornai, J. (1990), *The Road to a Free Economy, Shifting From a Socialist System: The Example of Hungary*, Norton, New York.

Le Grand, J. & Estrin, S., eds. (1989), *Market Socialism*, The Clarendon Press, Oxford.

Nuti, D.M. (1988), 'Competitive Evaluation and Efficiency of Capital Investment in the Socialist Economy', *European Economic Review*, Vol. 3, No. 2.

Nuti, D.M. (1989), 'Remonetization and Capital Markets in the Reform of Centrally Planned Economies'. Prepared for the LSE Financial Markets Group Conference on 'New Financial Markets: Economic Reform in Eastern Europe', 13 December, mimeo.

Swiecicki, M. (1988), 'Reforma Wlasnosciowa' (Ownership Reform). A paper for the seminar on 'Transformation Proposals for the Polish Economy', SGPiS, Warsaw, 17-18 November, mimeo.

Walters, K.D. & Monsen, R.J. (1983), 'Managing the Nationalized Company', *California Management Review*, Vol. 25, No. 4, pp. 16-27.

Winiecki, J. (1990a), 'No Capitalism Minus Capitalists', *Financial Times*, 20 June.

Winiecki, J. (1990b), 'Post-Soviet-Type Economies in Transition: What Have We Learned From the Polish Transition Programme in its First Year?', *Weltwirtschaftliches Archiv*, Vol. 126, No. 4, pp. 765-790.

7 The coping state: Shaping the institutional infrastructure

Introduction

'Economics is about a game within rules. Choices are made by actors ... constrained within specifically determined "laws and institutions" ' (Buchanan, 1979). Nowhere are we reminded about this dictum more clearly than in East-Central Europe, trying to shift to the market economy, while facing the painful lack of basic institutions of the market. General rules are often absent, market organizations nonexistent, policy instruments seriously underdeveloped—with adverse impact on the performance of economic agents and the economy as a whole.

In spite of strenuous efforts, supply of the institutional infrastructure is much too low relative to the demands of the 'workable' market economy, let alone the efficient one. The gap can diminish only with the passage of time—and many laws, the very absence of which limits the benefits of the stabilization and liberalization programmes now in operation in these countries.

This paper starts by reminding the reader of the type of economic institutions inherited from the Soviet-type economy and of the rather limited usefulness of those few that can be transformed into market institutions. Next, it deals with the areas of institution building where this activity has been most intensive in the early transition period.

What the present writer tries to signal in that section is the interplay of 'getting the prices right', which all stabilization cum liberalization programmes are about, and institution building. For it has sometimes been erroneously assumed that the former is a short run and the latter a long run problem. Even the short run requires 'getting (at least some of) the institutions right' to create the room for effective use of policy instruments in the (short run) adjustment. And these needs of getting macroeconomic policy-related institutions right dictate to a large extent the institution-building agenda of the executive and the legislature. The third section of the paper underlines the role of time, which emerges as the scarcest factor in the transition process. Two case studies are presented to show how important institution-building outcomes bring about only limited effects owing to the interdependence of various market institutions. Lack of specific rules within a given area or general rules in a linked area may nullify or severely limit the expected benefits of otherwise radical market-type measures. The gap between the demand for and supply of institutions can be narrowed only by the passage of time.

In the last section the main themes are reconsidered and certain conclusions drawn with respect to East-Central European experience in comparison with other transition cases. The advantaged of restoring distorted institutions over building new ones from scratch are stressed. Also, the relative importance of the set of well developed market institutions obtained by Eastern Germany as a result of reunification is underlined. This is seen as more important than the financial resource flow commonly regarded as the source of advantage of the former G.D.R. over other post-Soviet-type economies of East-Central Europe. In both cases it is institutions that ensure smoother transition and earlier benefits of higher efficiency.

Institutional Legacy of the Soviet Economic System

Throughout its history the Soviet economic system displayed major deficiencies that led to its decline and, as these deficiencies became more and more painful over time, finally to its demise. These deficiencies stemmed from problems that were unsolvable with the Soviet-type economy (STE) institutional setting. This setting made the Soviet or any other socialist system as envisaged by the classics a sure loser in the long run competition with the market alternative. This central insight of Ludwig von Mises ([1920], 1936) has for quite a few decades been lost to modern minds.

Centralisation of economic decision making generated unwieldy mammoth organisations (the well known planning pyramid from the textbooks on economics of planning, see, e.g., Ellman, 1989) and less well recognised lateral influences of the communist party apparatus (Winiecki, 1987, 1991a). The former had to cope unsuccessfully with the 'knowledge problem'—in the Michael Polanyi/Friedrich von Hayek sense (Lavoie, 1985)—while the latter added to continuous disturbances resulting from central planners' inevitable ignorance and their crude plan correction measures by political compaigns and *ad hoc* interventions.

The biggest loser was economic agents' initiative, entrepreneurship and innovativeness. Whatever was left of them was used outside the framework of aggregate wealth creation, which is what economic activity is mostly about. Avoidance of contradictory rules, innovative padding of enterprise and other organizations' reports, obtaining plan indicators that were easiest to implement and collecting resources that ensured this easy plan implementation (regardless of costs) became the major areas of economic agents' initiative.

The foregoing points to another unsolvable problem of the old institutional setting, namely the 'incentive problem'. Central planners and their political masters made extremely costly mistakes not only because of their inevitable ignorance stemming from the impossibility of obtaining the incommunicable, tacit knowledge residing in hundreds of thousands of economic agents, and not only because of the fact that by centralized price setting they destroyed the informational content of market prices (for economic agents reveal their partly tacit knowledge through their actions, which in turn affect prices).

Their mistakes were compounded by the fact that even that part of knowledge that has been communicable reached them in a highly distorted shape owing to the fact that economic agents' incentives severed the link between inefficient performance and reward. For it turned out that there is a world of difference between being paid for what one sells on the market and what one reports to one's superiors in the multilevel hierarchy. Agency costs (in the sense of Jensen & Meckling, 1976) turned out to be exorbitant in state-owned enterprises (SOEs), especially under the conditions of measurement without markets (Szymanderski & Winiecki, 1989, Winiecki, 1991a).

This, in turn, leads us to the third unsolvable problem, i.e. the 'property rights' problem'. The degree of control over management in the Soviet system, in spite of the ability of the rulers (central planners and their political overseers) to impose the heaviest possible penalties, including imprisonment, was only formally absolute. In terms of the ability to generate expected behaviour it has been a continuous fiasco.

Neither control over the flow of real resources in and out of enterprises by the multilevel planning hierarchy nor over the flow of financial resources by the monobank helped very much in the face of strong informational asymmetry between higher-level bureaucracies and enterprise managers in favour of the latter. Since the flow of financial resources has always been subordinated to the planned flow of goods and production factors, the monobank that was designed as a control body ended up as a mere cashier paying for whatever real resource flow took place in the economy—all the more so as *ad hoc* interventions of planners and apparatchiks protecting their rents in various enterprises added to the traditional concerns of planners with quantitative output targets that made them validate most unplanned cost increases (Winiecki, 1989a, 1991a). Thence stemmed the well known 'soft' budget constraints of SOEs under Soviet socialism (Kornai, 1979 and 1986).

Thus, the substitution of centralised decision making for the market incentive to produce and state ownership for private ownership with transferable property right made the much desired control over the economy impossible. Decisions were invariably costly and resulted in persistent excess demand, shortages and uncertainty. Centralization of decisions and wrongly structured incentives additionally ensured that the quantities produced with such fanfare (and much overstated figures) were of low quality and technologically obsolescent.

Tinkering with the system, which started already in the 1950s, was aimed at alleviating institutional deficiencies already visible at that time. The failure of tinkering—or at best marginal improvements—suggested unsolvability of the problems in question but at the time it was taken as evidence of growth problems. However, as an old East European joke had it, problems of growth were followed by the growth of problems. The story of how the Soviet economic system began to unravel is not of primary importance here, though.

What matters is that tinkering with the system under the name of economic reform tried to inject some bits and pieces of the market, at times—as in Hungary after 1968—with the effect of parallel existence of direct planners' commands and indirect inducements of economic policy. However, until the very end, the latter were subordinated to the former. Whenever problems cropped up, policy measures were held in abeyance, while commands (direct or in the guise of 'recommendations') got the upper hand. This situation made Janusz Beksiak (1988) call nominally autonomous reformed socialist enterprises 'enterprises until further orders'.

Indispensable Market Institutions and Requirements of Macroeconomic Policy

Our brief overview of the major deficiencies of the Soviet system at the same time draws the contours of the area in need of institution building. Governments in all post-Soviet-type economies face the same problem of filling the contours with the institutions (general rules, organisations, policy instruments) indispensable to the normal functioning of the market system. It is manifestly obvious that these institutions cannot be created overnight (all the more so as the political system is also in a state of transition and its ability ot tackle some more complicated issues of establishing—or in some cases reestablishing market institutions may be limited).

The difficulties of countries such as Poland, Hungary and Czecho-Slovakia (the only post-Soviet-type economies at the time of writing) are enormous. Almost all aspects of economic activity require immediate attention, almost all require new laws, institutions and policy measures. But only a few issues at a time can command the attention of governments coping with the resistance of inherited institutions (on information-processing capacity, see Simon, 1987). For it is the government which discovers this resistance in its attempts at facilitating the transition that is the main source of institution building initiative at the early stage. Those who raise doubts as to the propriety of such a road to the market should remember the saying of James Buchanan (1979) already quoted. Friedrich von Hayek also expected 'general rules' to be set by the state (1973). And in most aspects post-Soviet-type economies lack even these basic general rules.

Thus, demand for market institutions is very great from the start, while supply—in spite of strenuous efforts—is of necessity lagging behind. Only time can narrow the gap (as shown in Figure 7.1). Major issues may have to be left unattended and—what is worse—steps taken already may not bring expected results because other related steps have not yet been accomplished owing to

Figure 7.1

Demand and Supply of Market Institutions

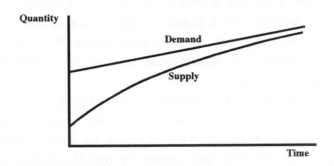

lack of time, underappreciation of the importance of some measures or simple neglect.

Supply of institution building by the government is determined not only by government's capacity to act but also by government's own needs in this respect. And these, leaving aside governments' theoretical persuasion and ideological preferences, are dictated to a large extent by their pressing need to cope with the inherited severe macroeconomic imbalances in the economy. That was the case in Poland, which was approaching hyperinflation at the time of political change in Autumn 1989, in Hungary, with its balooning foreign debt and an unbalanced economy facing 20-30% annual inflation, and in Czecho-Slovakia, although the imbalances in the latter were smaller than in Hungary (to say nothing about Poland). Nowhere else does the term 'coping state' (Hirschman, 1981) find better reflection than in the activities of both executive and legislature in post-Soviet-type economies trying to build from scratch the rudiments of the market.

The pressing need to equilibrate the economy in transition to the market requires some minimum room for macroeconomic policy and, as it turned out, it is in this area that governments concentrate their attention with respect to institution building. Thus, monetary policy requires as a first step the liquidation of the monobank and the creation of two-tier banking. This does not give it the room it has (for good or bad) in mature market economies but at least it gives the central bank an instrument with which to institute stringent monetary policy. In so doing it has to rely almost exclusively on a positive real central bank discount rate, given the nonexistence of the open market for short term government securities (an institutional task to be undertaken in some unspecified future).

Poland and Hungary were fortunate to an extent by the fact that communist reformers split the monobank into central bank and commercial banks in their last years of rule in both countries in question. Since the 'soft' budget constraint ruled supreme, central bank policies and credit expansion by commercial banks were severely distorted but at least the organizational rearrangements had already been made and some knowledge as to the proper behaviour of banking officials acquired by the personnel (even if not necessarily put into practice).

Czecho-Slovakia was not so fortunate and had to create two-tier banking after the political change. This, however, was countervailed by the lesser imbalances in the Czecho-Slovak economy, which allowed the government to devote more attention to various institutional measures.

Incidentally, the Polish cum Hungarian versus Czecho-Slovak case shows the ambiguous role of reform of—or tinkering with—the Soviet economic system. On the one hand, reform that resulted in decentralization of decision making without simultaneously linking decision making to capital risk (that is without change in property rights) generated stronger inflationary pressures, as rightly stressed by Vaclav Klaus (1990). On the other the very existence of previously misused institutions (phoney commercial banks, phoney bonds or no less phoney stock market) in the radically changed conditions of real transition to the market cuts the time needed to establish them and make them operate with a modicum of efficiency. Therefore earlier tinkering brings not only costs but also benefits (the latter mostly after the demise of the Soviet system, though).

A modicum of efficiency is probably as much as these newly established or adapted institutions can contribute in the early transition period. Although in the case of two-tier banking the discount rate becomes the main policy instrument of the central bank, complementary instruments from the old institutional setting are still used in parallel (refinancing credit as the only source of credit expansion for most commercial banks, credit rationing, etc.).

Furthermore, the very fact that commercial banks, albeit separated, are still state-owned organisations makes them behave more like bureaucracies than businesses. Thence stems mostly the high tolerance of mutual indebtedness among SOEs in both Poland and Hungary (and now increasingly in Czecho-Slovakia). This has been taking place in spite of the fact that in many cases delayed payments are so much higher than delayed receipts that they cannot conceivably be covered by cash flow. Yet banks continue to tolerate that situation and their willingness to act decisively, i.e. to refuse further credits to such SOEs, may not increase rapidly before they are privatized (yet another urgently needed institution building measure!).

Concern with the minimum necessary room for monetary policy is coupled with similar concern for fiscal policy. Here, too, certain institutional measures have to be undertaken to allow it to play its role in equilibrating the economy. These institutional changes also occupied much attention from the very beginning of the transition process.

On the revenue side, balancing the budget (a problem for all three governments but, again, most urgent for Poland) required first of all tightening of tax payment discipline, as well as curtailment of the plethora of tax reliefs. Although this task could be treated as another part of making the 'soft' budget constraint of enterprises harder (a policy measure), it should not be forgotten that the shift to the market-type policy measures required other measures that would equalise conditions for regimes (institutional measures). Thus, quite apart from the universal long-term aim of introducing VAT, interim tax measures that aimed at creating more equal conditions for competing enterprises also occupied government's attention.

On the expenditure side, substantial reduction of subsidies, greater tax discipline and significantly tighter monetary policy— all taken together—brought to the fore the question of unemployment and, consequently, institutions able to deal with the emerging problem. Employment offices, the heritage of the old system, were originally designed as institutions controlling the flow of labour, just as the monobank was designed as an instrument controlling the flow of money, and failed for the same reason. Here again government's scarce time had to be occupied with institutional measures: devising general rules of unemployment benefits, extending the area of responsibility of employment offices, devising crash training programmes for personnel of these offices, etc.

It is the considered opinion of the present writer that even allowing for the pressure of time on government performance, all governments so far failed in this respect (also sowing the germs of discontent with their actions in other areas than the level and structure of unemployment benefits, the availability and design of retraining schemes, etc.).

Obviously, making room for economic policy, i.e. indirect instruments influencing actions of economic agents (in contrast to planning directives) required as a prerequisite domestic price liberalisation. The extent of free prices has been a focus of intense attention owing to prices' role in the 'shock therapy' devised. Although a large part of price freeing decisions did not require changing rules, some decisions did, such as for example housing maintenance pricing. Pricing decisions in these areas were, however, usually postponed in the early transition period.

Creating the room for foreign economic policy required even more institutional measures. The choice of foreign exchange regime (everywhere fixed, adjustable exchange rates), the extent of currency convertibility, whether economic agents should have the right to maintain accounts in both domestic and foreign currencies, as well as trade policy-related measures (customs duties and their structure, tariff exemptions, export restrictions and import quotas, tax refunds), all required extensive elaboration of new rules.

Altogether the needs of adjustment—and adjustment by market-type measures at that—required not only policy decisions, i.e. choices within rules, but also institution building, i.e. choices among rules (see Buchanan, 1979, on the latter). Pressing needs of stabilization coupled with clearly stated preferences for liberalization and—within that large area—governments' perceived needs for effective policy instruments for short term adjustment, dictated to a large extent the actual content of the supply of institutional measures. Demand in other areas (privatization, demonopolization) has been left unsatisfied—or at least much less has been done there.

However, not only choice among areas but also that within areas was affected as much by the scarcity of time as by anything else. Some institutional measures required further institution building to reap fully (and sometimes to reap at all!) the efficiency benefits of the market system. It is for this reason that benefits of the shift to a market system grow incrementally rather than on a once-for-all basis—and this in spite of the 'shock therapy' introducing a critical mass of necessary policy and institutional measures in a short time span.

What is badly needed is a recognition of the fact that although wide ranging—and often painful—measures are put together in a package right at the start of the transition, this in no way means that efficiency and, accordingly, efficiency-based benefits will also be forthcoming in a large chunk shortly thereafter. For the critical mass of measures is a minimum necessary to get the ball rolling (Winiecki, 1989c), while benefits accumulate over time only, as the buildup of market institutions moves up along the supply curve, narrowing considerably the gap between demand for an supply of these institutions.

Unfortunately, governments in post-Soviet-type economies have been guilty to a smaller or larger extent of underappreciating the importance of the foregoing difference. This stemmed partly form the general lack of experience with the transition to the market and resultant ignorance of some related difficulties (such as the one-off fall in output early in the transition, see Chapter 1, and Winiecki, 1990 and 1991b), partly from the underappreciation of the time factor mentioned earlier and partly from the temptation to 'sell' the stabilization and systemic change programmes more easily to the general public by promising early improvements in living standards—early meaning measured in months rather than years. The political costs of succumbing to such temptation have been very serious.

Time as the Scarcest Factor in Interdependent Institution Building

Leaving aside the contributions of ignorance and policy mistakes, time emerged as the most scarce factor in institution building aimed at achieving higher efficiency associated with the shift to the market system. Two case studies illustrate the point. They show how benefits of choosing the right set of rules remain unrealised owing to the linkages between the newly established general rules and other (conflicting, linked or as yet nonexistent but necessary) rules, as well as nonexistent but necessary organizations.

Both cases deal with the most important component of long run changes, that is privatization. The first deals with privatization proper, that is the transfer of state assets into private hands (regardless of the chosen method—or methods—of privatization). The privatization law that by now has been passed in all three post-Soviet-type economies required a lot of work in each country but it represented only the tip of the iceberg of institution building associated with privatisation.

One of the issues that emerged while working on the privatisation bill in each country in question has been reprivatisation, that is the return of assets to their former owners. The issues has been extremely complex owing to the different legal status of earlier nationalizations (and sometimes no legal status whatsoever!), as well as the different 'recognizability' of nationalized assets (there is a big difference between assets that can be returned, like a pharmacy taken away from its owner in a house that still exists, and those that have to be valued somehow, since a factory, for example, may have become ten times bigger in the meantime).

Two different problems emerged. The first has been the elaboration of general rules of reprivatization/compensation (the latter in cases where reprivatization was thought desirable but impracticable). The second was not of institutional but psychological nature. Since uncertainty generated by claims of former owners cast a shadow over the legal status of some enterprises, their privatization would have to be delayed. These problems have so far been best solved in the Czecho-Slovak privatization bill by giving former owners of industrial assets compensation in the form of extra investment coupons, with which to bid for shares in privatized enterprises. The return of small pieces of landed property to their former owners is in the process of being solved by establishing proper rules everywhere, albeit not without problems.

Coupled with reprivatization and privatization claims are also those of lessees who during recent periods of communist reform acquired long term leases on state property and converted it (often at a substantial cost) into fashionable shops, restaurants, etc. Now their claims may conflict with those of former owners and those of, say, employees who are sometimes given the right to buy or lease shops in which they worked. These individual claims and counterclaims are only a part of the larger problem of the unsolved legal status of nationalized land, buildings, etc.

Interdependence with other general rules is better visible in the case of the separation of state property from that of municipal and other local authorities. In Poland, for instance, any privatization of shops, restaurants, etc., had to wait until the parliament passed the law on municipal authorities and municipal property. Only with the passage of that law were the municipal authorities that came into being after forty years of communist centralization able legally to take decisions on the sale or lease of municipal property. However, before an actual sale happened they had to establish clear property rights in the case of each particular piece of property.

These problems may, however, look minor in the face of the daunting task of privatizing a couple of thousand state-owned enterprises. Whatever the method of privatization (pure sale of assets as in Hungary, mixed sale cum free distribution of assets as in Poland, or prevailing free distribution in Czecho-Slovakia), the institutional requirements of practical conduct of the task are very extensive.

They are most extensive in the case of privatization by public sale of shares. Financial markets in post-Soviet-type economies are rudimentary at best. To be able to privatize so many enterprises, these economies (beside large savings of their populations) need a variety of financial institutions: investment banks, financial consultants, auditing firms, underwriters, etc.) able to value other privatization-related financial services. These institutions did not exist before (or at the very least not since 1945) and therefore there is a need of extending the banking law in order to cover also other types of banking firms than commercial banks. Charters for various financial professions have to be written as well. Thus, further sets of rules have to be elaborated, discussed and finally passed by the respective parliaments before privatization can start to any significant extent.

In any case, in this author's opinion, privatisation of thousands of enterprises by public sale would take decades if not centuries (Winiecki, 1989c; Gruszecki & Winiecki, 1991). This is true regardless of the speed with which the laws on various aspects of financial markets are passed or the number of actual financial firms being established.

A speedier alternative, i.e. free distribution of state property to the public, also needs further institution building, however, over and above the law on privatization and (in both cases) the stock market. Since only a part (and a small one at that) of the population would be both willing and able to select enterprises for the shares of which they would decide to bid, financial institutions are needed that would collect investment coupons from those who would prefer professionals doing the selection for them. The most suitable candidates seem to be mutual funds (Gruszecki & Winiecki, 1991) but for this, again, the status, rights and obligations of mutual funds need to be defined—again through the extension of the banking law. This, too, will slow down the process of privatization and, accordingly, the increase in efficiency expected from privatization.

Last but not least, the machinery of privatization has to be set up, i.e. the organization responsible for the administrative side of the whole operation. As has been shown by a much more limited free distribution case in Canada (the large state-owned corporation in British Columbia), this task is time and resource-consuming (see, Ohashi, 1980).

Thus, even privatisation 'shortcuts' such as free distribution among the population require a sequence of institution building measures that have to be put in place before the whole operation starts. All this requires time of the executive and the legislature.

The foregoing considerations concern what is sometimes called privatization 'from above', to stress the role of the state, setting the institutional framework for the transfer of its assets. An alternative to it is the privatization 'from below', i.e. the formation and expansion of private firms legally established as such from the start. They complement one another in altering the proportions between private and state sectors in the economy.

A natural reaction to the failed centralization of the Soviet economic system and simultaneously a recipe for freeing people's initiative should be the passage of a 'charter of economic freedom' allowing anybody to undertake any business activity subject to well defined limitations. The elaboration and passage of such a law is not very difficult under the changed political conditions: in fact, such a law was passed in Poland already toward the end of the period of rule of the last communist government.

Welcome as this embodiment of economic freedom has been, this is again only a beginning of the institutional story. It did release entrepreneurial activity in Poland where, after the passage of this law, the rate of formation of new, overwhelmingly private firms shot up. The same happened in Czecho-Slovakia, where during the first nine months of 1990 a quarter of a million small businesses were established (in spite of the lack of familiarity owing to the 40 years ban on private business activity in that country).

Yet Polish and Hungarian private businessmen complain about various sectoral and occupational regulations from the bygone era that are still in force and hamper their activity. Again, administrative action is necessary to reveal such obstacles and quite often it has to be followed by legislative action.

The foregoing, however, will still give people only the right to take initiatives. However, important after years of limitations and outright prohibitions, this nonetheless does not in any way increase the probability of success. To illustrate the point let us quote the example of Poland, where in the 1976-1986 period the average size of the private industrial firm in terms of employment increased form 1.6 to 2.6 persons per firm (and the statistics include owners as well!).

Obviously under communist regimes the private sector, if at all permitted, was allowed to exist but not to expand. Beside legal limitations there was also a lack of financial institutions geared to the needs of small private firms, artisans, etc. And for the existing monobanks private firms were the last priority. Now, legal restrictions are gone but the network of institutions supporting the expansion of the small business sector does not exist yet.

What this sector needs is small business development banks, insurance companies oriented toward naturally riskier small businesses, venture capital institutions, innovation centres encouraging risk taking by sharing the cost of developing new products and processes, etc. Without such institutional support post-Soviet-type economies will display a highly distorted size structure of firms: a large number of very large and large enterprises (privatized or not) and a sea of minuscule firms, too small ever to be able to become reliable suppliers of products and services to larger firms, and scarcely any intermediate size firms.

In all areas of financial markets, and in many other areas as well, there is a pressing need for Western expertise. However, in the case of fundamentally important institutional conditions for the growth of the private sector in post-Soviet-type economies there is also a possibility of going beyond technical assistance.

This author is generally sceptical about the effects of public financial assistance. The experience of bilateral and multilateral assistance to developing countries by and large supports this scepticism. Nonetheless, judiciously injected 'seed' money may in well considered cases do a lot of good. Building the network of institutions supporting the growth of the private sector belongs to that category. Instead of supporting, e.g., large industrial projects, Western bilateral and multilateral donors would do much better by using a fraction of the money to endow such newly established financial institutions with the badly needed initial capital, as well as to supply them with Western expertise (e.g. retired executives who would run these institutions for 3-5 years, while simultaneously training their local successors).

Of course, even without this network of supporting organisations some private firms would grow fast (and some of them did grow fast in Hungary and Poland in the last two years). But in order to make this phenomenon economically significant, that is, to obtain strong spillover effects of increasing vitality, size and efficiency of the private sector, these institutions are absolutely necessary. Otherwise, the benefits of shifting to a market system will remain limited for years to come. And it is the limited extent of the benefits—in stark contrast with heavily front-loaded costs! —that are the main source of public discontent.

Reconsiderations and Conclusions in Comparative Institutional Perspective

The previous two sections of this paper dwelled at some length on a series of interrelated themes. The first of these themes stressed that, in shaping the institutional infrastructure of the market, governments in post-Soviet-type economies have of necessity concentrated on certain priority areas. Institutions creating the rudimentary framework that makes post-STEs responsive to macroeconomic policy measures, as well as those creating the basic framework for future integration with the world market (and responsiveness to stimuli coming from that market have been in the centre of attention. The rationale for this concentration stemmed from large and quickly growing internal and external imbalances in the pre-transition stage that required concentration of efforts on these areas.

Since monetary and fiscal measures, coupled with liberalisation of domestic prices and liberalization of foreign trade and payments, constitute the core of all stabilization cum liberalization programmes, these priorities were generally regarded as acceptable. Other areas in need of institution building got less attention, although it is worth stressing that in Czecho-Slovakia work on privatization has been advancing almost simultaneously with institutional changes in the monetary and fiscal, as well as foreign economic policy areas.

This is not surprising. Having inherited the least disequilibrated economy among former socialist countries, the Czecho-Slovak government could devote less attention—in relative terms—to re-

194

storing some measure of equilibrium (and introducing related institutional changes) and more to other areas in need of market institutions. This is not intended to mean that macroeconomic stabilisation was neglected. On the contrary, in the pre-transition year of 1990 the money stock grew in nominal terms by 1-2%, while prices increased sharply, especially in the fourth quarter. The budget deficit was also sharply cut.

The second theme concerned the interrelatedness of institutional change both within and between various areas of the economy. The necessity of building market institutions from scratch meant that the lack of institutions in one area (e.g. the law on public property separating state from municipal and local authorities' property) constrained institution building elsewhere (here, change in the property rights structure, that is privatization). Also, certain general rules, e.g. those establishing fundamental economic freedom, require—in order to release entrepreneurial activity —an extensive review of many existing industry-specific and real property-related laws with the aim of removing obstacles to entrepreneurship.

Furthermore, it was stressed that possibilities, in order to become realities, need institutional support in the form of a network of institutions geared to the needs of a dynamically growing small business sector. It is, however, the opinion of the present writer that governments of all post-Soviet-type economies not only did not give priority to this type of institution building (which is not surprising) but also plainly underestimated its importance. It is one thing to keep an issue on the back burner for the time being, given the crowded agenda (see Simon, 1987) and another to underestimate the importance of the issue.

The foregoing interrelatedness of various institution building measures strongly affected the performance of these economies in the early phases of transition to the market. Demand for institutions needed to establish a 'workable', that is relatively efficiently functioning market economy has been not only highly but also 'inelastic' (in the sense that a certain critical mass of institutions is necessary to get the ball rolling). But supply of institutions, policy mistakes aside, has been primarily constrained by capacities of both governments and parliaments to elaborate necessary measures. Rephrasing the well-known Kornai term, post-Soviet-type economies turned out to be supply-constrained as far as market institutions are concerned—at least in the short-to-medium run.

The third theme concerned the efficiency (and welfare) effects of institutional changes lagging behind the needs of a 'workable' market economy. Without the needed critical mass of market institutions, benefits of the shift to the market system could be reaped to a limited extent only. For there is a difference between a critical mass of macroeconomic policy and liberalization measures that together form a stabilization cum liberalization programme and the critical mass of market institutions that create a 'workable' market economy. Only the latter (preceded, of course, by the former) brings large benefits from distinctly higher efficiency.

The difference between the former and the latter is known in the literature under the different terminology of forced and fundamental adjustment. It is the undistorted, well working market institutions that ensure the economy's ability to adjust in both a static and a dynamic sense. Without these institutions only the former effect can be achieved. Unfortunately, understanding of the differences outlined here has been rather limited.

This was the source of a lot of confusion and disappointment. After the 'big bang', the radical change of economic regime, after large costs at the start of the transition, the benefits of the market system were for many surprisingly slow in coming. The disappointment has been often aggravated by the fact that governments often set unrealistically short time horizons for promised improvements in living standards.

The Polish government, for example, announced in its programme that visible improvement would begin as soon as the second half of 1990. This can be compared with the more realistic expectation of the authors of the programme of stabilization and systemic change prepared at about the same time at the request of the parliamentary club of 'Solidarity', where the improvement in living standards was expected to take place after the completion of the programme, i.e. after the 1991 (see Beksiak, Gruszecki, Jedraszczyk & Winiecki, 1990). The Hungarian government, distancing itself from the 'big bang' approach, also made some unrealistic promises. At the time of writing both had paid for that at the ballot box and beyond.

In conclusion the present writer would like to stress a point that may seem quite obvious but certainly was not (at least not for everybody) at the beginning of the transition programmes in post-Soviet-type economies. It is much easier to restore distorted but nonetheless existing market institutions than to build them from scratch. Accordingly, the effects of stabilization and liberalization programmes in countries with distorted markets are often visible much sooner and are initially markedly larger than in countries without markets, where missing but interdependent institutions lower the effects of the measure already undertaken.

Therefore, the easy optimism of some Western experts based on the experience of Latin American and Asian countries may seem unfounded. Differences of opinion concern less the choice of measures of their sequence than the time horizon of the expected higher level of efficiency thanks to the shift to the market system after the measures have been undertaken.

A second conclusion, also put in comparative perspective, concerns the prospects of post-STEs in East-Central Europe *vis-à-vis* that of Eastern Germany. The usual argument underpinning much more optimistic expectations with respect to the latter is the financial might of Western Germany, the billions of Deutchmarks that are flowing and will be flowing eastward in years to come.

This reasoning the present writer regards as very narrowly focussed. Financial resource flows matter, especially where they make it easier to bear the social consequences of a very rapid transition to the market. But what matters even more is the fact that Eastern Germany, instead of hectically building the rudiments of the market system from scratch and for some time without visible effects in terms of marked improvements in efficiency, as Hungary, Poland or Czecho-Slovakia have to, got at the start all the institutions of the market economy in already well developed (because tried and tested) form. To this we must add law and order, a stable currency and—last but not least—the pooling of risk, given the much larger size of Western Germany. It is these much less often mentioned institutional benefits of the former G.D.R. which East-Central European countries can capture only with great effort—and in the longer run at that.

References

Beksiak, J. (1988), 'On Authentic and Socialist Enterprises'. A paper presented at a seminar on 'Transformation Proposals of Polish Economy', Warsaw, SGPiS, 17-18 November, 1988 (in Polish).

Beksiak, J., Gruszecki, T., Jedraszczyk, A. & Winiecki, J. (1990), 'Outline of a Programme for Stabilisation and Sytemic Change', in The Polish Transformation: Programme and Progress, Centre for Research into Communist Economies, London, July.

Buchanan, J.M. (1979), *What Should Economists Do?*, Liberty Press, Indianapolis.

Ellman, M. (1989), *Socialist Planning*, second edition, Cambridge University Press, Cambridge.

Gruszecki, T. & Winiecki, J. (1991), 'Privatisation in East-Central Europe: A Comparative Perspective', *Aussenwirtschaft*, No. 1.

Hayek, F. von (1973), *Law, Legislation and Liberty*, Vol. 1: *Rules and Order*, Routledge and Kegan Paul, London.

Hirschman, A.O. (1981), *Essays in Trespassing - Economics to Politics to Beyond*, Cambridge University Press, Cambridge.

Jensen, M.C. & Meckling, W.H. (1976), 'Theory of the Firm: Managerial Behavior, Agency Costs and Ownership Structure', *Journal of Financial Economics*, Vol. 3, No. 4.

Klaus, V. (1990), 'Political and Economic Reform in Eastern Europe: A Case of Czechoslovakia'. A paper prepared for The Mont Pelerin Society general Meeting 'Europe in an Open World Order', Munich, 2-8 September, mimeo.

Kornai, J. (1979), 'Resource-Constrained versus Demand-Constrained Systems', *Econometrica*, Vol. 47, No. 4.

Kornai, J. (1986), 'The Soft Budget Constraint', Kyklos, Vol. 39, No. 1.

Lavoie, D. (1985), *National Economic Planning, What Is Left?*, Ballinger, Cambridge, Mass.

Mises, L. von [1920] (1935), 'Economic Calculation in the Socialist Commonwealth', in Hayek, F. von, ed., *Collectivist Economic Planning: Critical Studies on the Possibilities of Socialism*, Routledge & Sons, London.

Ohashi, T.M. 'Privatization in Practice: The Story of the British Columbia Resources Investment Corporation', in Ohashi, T. and Roth, T.P., *Privatization in Theory and Practice*, The Fraser Institute, Vancouver.

Simon, H.A. (1987), 'Politics as Information Processing', *LSE Quarterly*, Vol. 1, No. 4.

Szymanderski, J. & Winiecki, J. (1989), 'Dissipation de la rente, managers et travailleurs dans le systeme sovietique: les implications pour un changement du systeme', *Revue d'etudes comparatives Est-Ouest*, Vol. 20, No. 1.

Winiecki, J. (1987), 'Why Economic Reforms Fail in the Soviet System. A Property Rights-Based Approach', Institute for International Economic Studies seminar paper No. 374, Stockholm, January, mimeo.

Winiecki, J. (1989a), 'Large Industrial Enterprises in Soviet-Type Economies: The Ruling Stratum's Main Rent-Seeking Area', *Communist Economies*, Vol. 1, No. 4.

Winiecki, J. (1989b), 'How To Get the Ball Rolling', *Financial Times*, 13 January.

Winiecki, J. (1989c), 'Privatizacion en las economias de tipo sovietico', *Estudios Economicos*, No. 4.

Winiecki, J. (1990), 'Heilsamer Druck. Ostreformen: Realistische Zahlen', *Wirtschaftswoche*, No. 44.

Winiecki, J. (1991a), *Resistance to Change in the Soviet Economic System*, Routledge, London.

Winiecki, J. (1991b), 'On Inevitability of Output Fall in Early Transition to the Market: Theoretical Underpinnings', *Soviet Studies*, Vol. 43, No. 4.